Shelton Publishing
2701 Weaver Hill Drive
Apex, NC 27502
www.coalmarch.com

Ordering Information:
Quantity sales. Special discounts are available on quantity purchases by corporations, associations, and others. For details, contact the publisher at the address above.

Publisher's Cataloging-in-Publication data
Shelton, Donnie.
BUILD: How to create a phenomenal team for your service company. / Donnie Shelton
p. cm.
Shelton Publishing
ISBN-13: 978-0-9996674-0-8 (Custom Universal)
1. Marketing. 2. Sales. 3. Business Development. 4. Management 5. Service Business Management

First Edition
1
Printed in the United States of America

TO EMILY, CAROLINE,
MAREN, BLAKE AND
OWEN. GRATITUDE IS THE
KEY TO HAPPINESS AND
I AM SO GRATEFUL FOR
EACH ONE OF YOU.

Contents

"There is a construct in computer programming called 'the infinite loop' which enables a computer to do what no other physical machine can do - to operate in perpetuity without tiring. In the same way it doesn't know exhaustion, it doesn't know when it's wrong and it can keep doing the wrong thing over and over without tiring."

- John Maeda

Introduction

Does This Sound Familiar?

From the outside, Bill appears to be nothing short of a stunning success. As a small service company owner, Bill lives in a nice home, drives the latest model truck, and owns an office building complete with the newest technology, finest leather couches, and a small army of employees. Bill's friends and family know him to be a hard worker with humble beginnings who has "made it". With no advanced degree and limited financial resources, Bill has built his service company to what it is today on nothing more than hard work and sheer dedication. His friends and family are even a little envious because Bill appears to have unbounded freedom and limitless financial resources.

Bill started his career as a service technician at a highly successful service company. Bill quickly rose through the ranks and became known as the go-to guy because he had excellent technical abilities and wonderful people skills. Bill consistently earned the highest sales and highest customer service satisfaction scores. He outworked and outperformed every other technician and was eventually promoted into management.

After outperforming his peers month after month, Bill began to critique his employer. There were so many mundane systems, so many procedures and oh so many checklists. Bill believed that the majority of these systems were unnecessary at best and a waste of time at worst. Plus, guys like him didn't need those things to get the job done. In Bill's mind, all those checklists and systems were for people with much less capacity and capability than him.

With his superior technical knowledge and sales ability, Bill eventually became disgruntled with his somewhat stoic and rigid employer and started his own service company. Bill knew that it would be a lot of work to start up his own business, but he dreamed of eventually making more money while also working fewer hours.

Now, 5 years later, at 6:10 a.m., Bill is heading to the office. Instead of living his dream of fewer hours and more money, he's barely surviving a nightmare of long days and high debt. Bill routinely works 10-12 hours a day and when he does go home, he can't be completely present. He's at home physically, but mentally the business and all of its problems are ever-present in his mind.

Bill's dream of more time hasn't panned out as he thought it would. This morning, as he pulls into the parking lot at the office, his mind is racing about his task list that he hasn't touched in over a month and his schedule full of back-to-back meetings. Bill knows that it's physically impossible to do all the things that he needs to get done today. Hell, it would take him three full days with no distractions just to clear his task list, not to mention all of the decisions that are waiting for his approval. What scares him the most, though, is the feeling of being overwhelmed and the sheer fact that he has felt this way each morning for the last 5 years.

Bill's dream of more money has evaporated too. Bill has had to take out credit lines to fund the operations of his business and he's resorted to using credit cards to pay the bills. Failed marketing campaigns and bloated payrolls have taken their toll on Bill's cash position and with his credit tapped out and no savings, Bill has to go to great lengths to ensure that he has enough cash to make payroll. Each week, by sheer strength and determination, Bill miraculously pulls it off – only to have the same issue the next payday.

When Bill worked for his previous employer, life seemed way simpler. He was busy, but somehow it seemed like a different busy, one that was a lot less stressful. He never had thoughts like, how can I possibly get everything done? How the hell am I going to make payroll next week? Will all of my employees show up today?

Why do I always seem to be short on money at the end of the month? What am I going to do about an employee that I know I need to fire but can't afford to lose right now?

Now that he owns his own company, questions like these never seem to go away.

CRITICAL QUESTIONS TO CONSIDER

The reality is that most small service companies operate just like Bill's company.

This is to say that most small service companies really don't work at all – their owners do. Day after excruciating day, these owners and managers drag themselves to a business that started out as a dream but quickly escalated into a nightmare. Each day is riddled with unmotivated and unproductive employees who show up late and leave early... if they even bother to show up at all.

Then there are the customer issues, the financial issues, the regulatory issues, and the issue list goes on and on. Problem after problem, headache after headache, year after year, the nightmare slowly sucks the life out of Bill and the other 90% of service company owners just like him.

Why is Bill's story such a common one?

Why is it that most service company owners live their lives like this? How is it that such talented people, for one reason or another, believe that by working more hours and borrowing more money that they can turn a nightmare back into the original dream they once had?

How is it that the minority of service company owners have businesses that provide them with the financial means to live the lifestyle that they desire with the time to actually enjoy their lives? How is it that after work these owners can go home and be fully present with their families with no worry of what's happening at their company or what might happen tomorrow?

What do the highly successful service company owners know that the ones suffering through a nightmare don't? Do these successful owners work harder? Do they have and invest more money? What's the difference?

The reality is that the successful service company owners don't work harder and they don't invest more money. Their businesses consistently kick off cash to them while requiring a minimal amount of their time.

Most service company owners like Bill are incredibly hard workers and talented people. The problem is that they are working hard and spending time on the wrong things in their business.

THE ESSENTIAL SKILL OF A SUCCESSFUL SERVICE COMPANY

If you own a service company or if you want to own a service company, then this book was written for you.

If you manage a service company or want a management role at a service company, then this book was written for you.

The reason that most service companies resemble Bill's is that fundamentally most owners and managers don't understand the single most powerful lever to building a successful service company. Many believe that by working harder and investing more (time and money) that they can turn things around and build a successful business.

I am here to tell you that this idea and these business owners are dead wrong.

Ask any service company owner what his or her greatest challenge is and I guarantee that invariably the conversation will revolve around people issues.

How can I make such a bold claim? Do I have some innate psychic or prophetic ability that others simply don't have? Nope.

The reality is that operating a service company is very different from owning and operating other types of businesses because it requires people to satisfy the needs of other people. It doesn't matter if your service is white collar or blue collar, for neither is immune to this fact. I've worked with companies with service offerings that span from emergency medical treatment to waste management and they all struggle with the same issue. People. They all have people issues.

The crazy thing is that even though almost every service company owner will tell you that people issues are their #1 problem, very few actually do anything about it. It's as if they're aware of the problem but find it easier to work themselves to death on other, less important priorities to avoid dealing with people. As a result, their businesses end up in chaos. These companies are unmanageable, unpredictable, and unfortunately for the owner, very unrewarding.

No service company is immune or exempt from people issues because to provide the service you must have people. And as people, we have imperfections as part of our nature. We're oftentimes emotional, inconsistent and irrational to the point of being a little bit crazy. That's just being human! It's simply who we are. It also happens to make building a successful service company particularly challenging.

The fact is that most service companies, just like Bill's company, struggle day after day, year after year because they simply don't understand the real work of building a successful service company. All you have to do is ask the owner: "what's your most important task?" Depending on the day, (heck, in some cases depending on the hour,) you'll hear things like: marketing, sales, operations, financial discipline, and the list goes on and on.

I'm here to tell you that it's none of those things. All of them are important, but at the end of the day, if you really want to build a successful service company, you only need one essential skill:

The ability to attract and retain the right people in your business.

When you think about it, of course marketing is important, of course sales are important, and of course operations are important; however, every single one of those things can be outsourced or handed off to a manager. Building and developing a great team, though, falls squarely on your shoulders.

For a moment, I want you to think about a highly successful service company owner that's lasted over the long term (meaning more than 10 years). What are their strengths? What about their weaknesses? I guarantee that the most successful owners and managers are those who know how to recruit the right people and then develop them once they have them in the door.

If you only get one thing from this book, get this: The most successful service company owners know how to recruit, train and develop the right people for their company, and that's what they spend their time doing. It's this skill that separates the successful owners from the Bills in your industry. It's this skill that solves your people issues.

THE BUILD™ FRAMEWORK

Who I am

I have walked in Bill's shoes (more than once). I've had money issues, people issues, and customer issues. On more than one night, I've been up at 3 a.m. worried about how I'd cover payroll. When I was growing my first service company, I had no investors and no cash reserves. I had to bootstrap my company and grow it on the money that I earned and the people skills that I had. I knew little to nothing about how to build and manage a team and boy did I make mistakes.

Armed with the popular dogma of "just be nice and people will work hard for you," I made just about every mistake that you can make with employees. As a result, I had employees steal from me, lie to me, cheat my customers, and, in one case, start his own business using my customer base.

In short, I'm not some "guru" or "consultant" who knows what you "should" be doing, but has never actually done it himself. I've lived the life of a service company owner and I continue to live it to this day. Even with all of its challenges, I love what I do. I'm one of the lucky ones who turned something that I enjoy doing – growing companies – into a career. To me, there's nothing more fun than setting seemingly impossible goals and then crushing them.

One of the biggest lessons I've learned in the trenches is that the key to success in business (and in life) is to view almost everything that you do as a system. Once you view your business as one giant set of connected, smaller systems, all you need to do is standardize and perfect them for your business to become fun, easy, and chaos-free (mostly). Best of all, you won't be Bill – your business will serve you.

This book focuses on the key system in your business that creates a successful service company: your people system. It describes a system that will allow you to accomplish what most others believe is impossible: to build a successful service company that provides you with more cash than Floyd Mayweather after a pay-per-view fight (ok maybe that's a stretch but you get the idea,) and the time to work on your tan in the Bahamas (if that's your thing).

The Build™ framework shows you how to leverage your most important asset, your people, to build a highly successful and rewarding business. You'll learn how not to be Bill by getting off the treadmill and making real progress in every area of your business.

Though I'd love to tell you otherwise, the truth is that the Build™ framework was developed more out of sheer necessity than managerial genius.

With this people system, I have grown two service companies to the multi-million dollar level in less than four years. Keep in mind that, in my industry, it takes an average of about ten years to reach the million dollar level. I've also helped hundreds of other business owners grow their companies using this same system with comparable results. These companies range in sector, location, and size. The system gets results.

Why I Decided to Write This Book

Since starting my first service company, countless other business owners have helped me immeasurably. The advice and knowledge that they shared with me has been literally worth millions of dollars. None of them ever asked for compensation, and all of them gave me their time and advice freely. I will forever be grateful to these business owners and friends who helped me along the way and I know I wouldn't be where I am today without their help.

I wrote this book because I don't want you to go through what I did in order to build a successful service company. I don't want you wasting time, money and your life on trying to solve the wrong problems.

My hope is that this book does for you what others have done for me. While it's great to learn from your own experience, sometimes it's better to learn from the experience of others.

The Build™ platform is the culmination of my experience and the experience of some of the owners I've worked with in building successful service companies. Over time, and after a few embarrassments, I've refined this system and feel that it's ready to share with you. But knowledge is only part of the equation – executing it is what brings results, and that's up to you.

I've seen the Build™ framework completely turn companies around and, in some cases, add over 20% more profit to their bottom line. By implementing the Build™ framework, you'll be one of the rare business owners who actually has money to live the lifestyle you desire with the time to enjoy it.

Fundamentally, you'll know how to build a team that can not only replace you, but also get better results than you ever could on your own. You'll experience less stress, make more money, and make a positive impact on many people. Building a successful business positively impacts your life – your team, your team's families, your customers, and, most importantly, your family. It's like winning a G6 on Oprah!

No matter what problems and challenges you're currently facing with your service company, I know that as you begin to implement the principles in the Build™ framework that your business will grow faster, become more profitable, and be much more enjoyable to operate.

So let's get to the business of learning about the Build™ framework and how to implement it into your company.

THIS BOOK HAS THREE SECTIONS:

Section 1

Section 1 is the foundation of Build™. It's about understanding the fundamental ideas and principles that the framework is built upon. It's about developing a mindset for both you and your team so you can extract the maximum value from your investment of time and money. Without understanding the principles of what it takes to build a great service company, any time spent implementing the Build™ framework will be an utter waste. John F. Kennedy once famously said, "efforts and courage are not enough without purpose and direction." Consider Section 1 the "purpose and direction" of the Build™ framework.

Section 2

Section 2 is the brass tacks of the Build™ framework. I show you how to recruit, hire, train and ultimately develop your people in your service company to extract both maximum value for the business and for you as the business owner. In this section I am going to show you exactly how to get started and provide you with worksheets to get you started.

Section 3

Section 3 guides you through best practices in implementing the Build™ framework. It shows you the common steps and the common pitfalls as you transform your service company.

"Experience is a hard teacher because she gives the test first, the lesson afterward."

- Vernon Law

Chapter 1

An Unfortunate Reality

As an 18-year-old, I sat across a table from an oral surgeon who advised me that if I was his son he'd recommend that I proactively remove my wisdom teeth. He then extolled upon me all of the benefits of not having those pesky wisdom teeth and how much "better" life would be without them even though I wasn't currently experiencing any issues. According to him, it was only a matter of time before I would start having problems, and plus, I was in the Air Force so this surgery would be completely free.

By the time he was done selling me on all of the benefits of the surgery, I viewed the procedure as a no-brainer. My then-18-year-old brain, as usual, gave no thought of the risks that might be involved because, in my mind, the surgeon was a professional and nothing could possibly go wrong. In fact, I don't recall even thinking that I might experience some pain, much less any complications from the surgery.

So with all of the wisdom of an 18-year-old, I immediately scheduled my proactive surgery to remove teeth that I was not having any issues with on the Thursday before Memorial Day weekend. My thinking was, get wisdom teeth removed Thursday, recover Friday, and still have the weekend for fun.

Once the surgery was complete, I woke up feeling great. I mean really great. If you don't know what I mean when I say "great" just YouTube "post wisdom teeth surgery" and you'll understand what I'm talking about. As the surgeon was leaving the room, he mentioned in passing how my wisdom teeth sure were "little rascals" to get out. At the time, I didn't give this statement much thought, though later on I realized that was code for "I just put a beat down on your mouth you just don't know it yet."

Once the effects of the drugs from the surgery wore off, I understood the "little rascals" comment with complete clarity. My head felt like it was going to split and there were sharp pains jolting down both sides of my jaw. As an added bonus, my face looked like a chipmunk that just had just binged on a tree of acorns after a long hibernation. It was at this point I realized that my idea of a quick recovery after surgery followed by a weekend of fun probably wasn't going to work out the way that I'd planned.

Thursday night was shaping up to be nothing like I'd envisioned.

Instead of just sleeping off the surgery, I ended up awake all night trying to find a way to dull the pain so I could go to sleep. Friday was no different. I was taking the meds that the surgeon prescribed and I was even devouring over-the-counter medications like they were Skittles, but nothing worked. Finally, at 1 a.m. on Saturday morning, I'd had enough.

I went to the on-base emergency room and described the pain that I was feeling and the fact that I had just had surgery the previous Thursday morning. The ER nurse took one look at me and said, "oh yeah, we handle this type of emergency all of the time. We'll get you fixed right up and have you out of here in no time." Little did I know that "no time" meant 5 hours later and "fixed right up" meant just numbing the pain.

Once the ER nurse was done with "fixing me right up" I went home and I was able to go to sleep as the pain was masked by the Novocain, but, once the numbness wore off, all of the pain that I felt before came right back. That weekend, I ended up repeating this same procedure Saturday night, Sunday night, and even Monday night. All visits followed the same routine. That is, I'd show up sometime after 12 a.m., I'd get numbed up, and I'd get discharged around 5 a.m. I would then sleep about 5 hours only to show up that same evening to do it all over again.

Finally, Tuesday came and I visited the clinic that completed the surgery. Within seconds the surgeon said, "well Donnie, you have dry socket on both sides of your jaw and a lot of infection. That must be very painful. Why didn't you have the ER doc call my emergency cell phone to get you treated? You shouldn't have waited this long to come see us!" Needless to say, I had no clue that such an option existed and the thought that I could have avoided the weekend from hell made me sick to my stomach. Within 30 minutes the oral surgeon performed a simple procedure that the ER docs never performed and I immediately began feeling better.

As it turns out, the ER docs who "dealt with this issue all of the time" and who would "fix me right up" never really understood what was happening with my jaw the entire time. In fact, the ER docs completely missed the source of my pain and instead focused only on resolving the immediate cause of pain by numbing me up. Each night I returned to the same ER, with the same ER nurses and same ER doctors, and no one even gave a second thought to the fact that I kept showing up with the same problem every night that weekend. What's even more baffling (and intriguing) is the fact that those doctors had a resource that they could have called on (e.g. the oral surgeon) but never did.

The tragedy of this entire experience was that the ER doctors and nurses were so focused on treating the symptoms no one ever stopped to question why the symptoms kept coming back. No one ever made the connection that numbing the pain wasn't actually helping. In fact, numbing me up was doing nothing more than masking the real problem (dry socket and infection) long enough for me to get some sleep. In the end, these docs focused on and preferred treating symptoms rather than doing the more difficult work of trying to determine the actual problem that was causing the symptoms. Furthermore, not one of them took the time to acknowledge that what they were doing was not working and that they needed to call the oral surgeon to get it resolved.

I could probably write an entire other book on the lessons that I learned from this experience, but I'll spare you and just focus on the most important one. What this experience drove home to me, in this most dramatic way, is that most people are perfectly fine living their lives treating symptoms rather than doing the more difficult job of identifying and resolving problems. In fact, most people don't want to bother with the difficult task of identifying problems because it's much, much easier to address symptoms. Think about it – diagnosing and resolving problems typically takes more time, more knowledge, more thought, and usually more work.

As a business owner who has grown multiple companies from nothing to the multi-million dollar level, I can tell you that most service company owners and managers are not very different than military ER docs. I've worked with hundreds of other service company owners and managers who are perfectly fine to treat the symptoms that their businesses are currently experiencing (employee issues, money issues, etc.) rather than take the time to think about what's actually the source problem that is causing the symptoms. In my experience, the vast majority of them want an easy solution to grow their business, manage their department or make more money without the hard and messy work of identifying the real problems in their businesses.

Most owners and managers believe that by resolving symptoms they're doing a great job in their role even though the same symptoms seem to arise again and again (a clear sign that the problem is not being addressed). The funny thing is that just like the ER docs, these owners and managers usually have the ability to get help with just a phone call or by reading a book, but most never take the time or make the effort to do so.

In the chapters that follow, we're going to go through what it takes to build a phenomenal service company. By phenomenal I mean a profitable, sustainable company that customers love to do business with and employees love to work for. First and foremost, if you really want to build a phenomenal company, you must understand a fundamental concept: always identify and treat problems, don't allow yourself to treat symptoms and call it good. The framework that's described later in this book is easy to understand but hard to implement. As you go through implementation you're going to find a lot of problems and also a lot of symptoms. Determine now that you'll spend your time resolving problems and not waste your time and effort on simply treating symptoms.

MOST OWNERS AND MANAGERS DON'T KNOW WHAT THEY'RE DOING

Before we had children, my wife, Emily, worked as a nurse at UNC hospitals in Chapel Hill, NC. After suffering through a couple of years of rotating shifts at the respiratory intensive care unit and a few near-miss accidents due to falling asleep at the wheel after an all night shift, my wife decided that she wanted to transition to a company and position where she had day working hours so that she could get more sleep and we could spend more time together.

Emily decided that she wanted to work for the best dermatologist in the Raleigh area. Ever so smart and studious, Emily set her sights on getting hired there and within one week she had a job offer.

The opportunity for Emily to work with this dermatologist was both overwhelming and exciting. Before her first day we talked at length about the opportunity and how much she'd learn. She was so excited to be working for this doctor and to be affiliated with such a cutting-edge practice. This dermatologist had been featured in multiple magazines and was the official dermatologist for the Carolina Hurricanes, Raleigh's professional hockey team.

After the first couple of weeks, Emily's enthusiasm and excitement turned into frustration. Even though the dermatologist was highly talented and well respected, his office was an absolute disaster. Day in and day out there were employees gossiping about each other, employee fights, employees calling in sick, employees showing up late, and employees not showing up at all. Indeed, the practice lacked basic structure and leadership and without either the inmates were running the asylum.

Six months later, Emily reported to work only to find the doors locked and chained shut. The landlord of the office building where the practice was located had literally chained the doors shut due to non-payment of rent by the doctor. According to the landlord, the rent had not been paid in over 9 months. This was a total and complete shock to the doctor (as he had assumed that all bills were getting paid,) and that morning the drama between him and the landlord unfolded in front of all of the employees.

As it turned out, the doctor was paying his bills. The only problem was that the payments were not making it to the actual vendors, but into the pockets of his office manager. With no office building to operate out of, and over 9 months of bills unpaid, the doctor closed the business and filed for bankruptcy.

After doing some research, Emily discovered that this was old hat for this doctor. This latest closure of his office was the 4th time in his 30 years of practice. Two months later he opened yet another practice and I bet you'll never guess who the office manager was? If you made a wild guess that it was the same employee who embezzled from him, you're correct. It seemed that she was sorry for what she'd done and convinced him that she'd be the perfect person to help with his new start in his next office. (Update: that office has since closed down as well.)

While this doctor was a gifted and well-respected dermatologist, he was an absolutely incompetent business owner. What's even more telling is that this experience and this story is not that uncommon in the health services industry. Doctors and dentists, while wonderful and knowledgeable technicians, are notorious for being horrible business owners and money managers.

How is it that people so smart, gifted, and talented can't seem to own and operate a business effectively? How is it that people that go through 5-8 years of postgraduate education can't seem to accomplish what many others have with no formal college experience?

The answer is as subtle as it is simple. When you think about it, how do most owners and managers come to be owners and managers of service companies?

The typical path to management and ownership in most service companies is through technical expertise. This is to say, that if a person is really good at performing the service (e.g. the technical work), whether that's treating patients in the ER or repairing a roof, the technician naturally gets promoted to manager because he or she is really good at doing the technical work of the business, or they decide to start their own company.

Most service company owners and managers completely miss one essential and critical fact:

Doing the work of a business is completely different than operating a business

As a result, most managers and owners are not leaders at all. They're nothing more than bonafide technicians who love doing the technical work of their service company and who promote other technicians. The end result is a company being led and managed by technicians who know nothing about operating a company and who aren't interested in learning the necessary skills, either.

Therein lies the problem. Symptoms of employee issues, financial issues, legal issues, etc., are usually nothing more than indicators of a service company that is being operated by technicians. The fact is that operating a company has nothing to do with the technical work of a business.

Think about that for a moment. Do you think the CEO of GE understands thermodynamics? What about the CEO of IBM? Think he understands how to write code that will embed artificial intelligence into a robot? What about the CEO of Southwest Airlines? Do you think he's flying the nonstop from Orlando to Raleigh?

What these CEOs know, and what all great company owners and managers know, is that the discipline of operating a company is completely different and separate from the technical work of the business and that operating a company requires just as much, if not more effort than doing the technical work of the company.

The issue is that most service company owners and managers start their careers doing technical work that their service company provides and when an owner becomes an owner or a manager becomes a manager, instead of acknowledging that they have to learn a completely new skill set (like managing people and operating a company), they instead go back to what they know best, the technical work.

MOST SERVICE COMPANIES DON'T WORK AT ALL

An unfortunate reality is that most small and medium-sized service companies are actually owned and managed by technicians who pretend to know what they're doing when, in fact, they don't have a clue.

These technician owned and managed businesses are easy to spot because every last one of them has employee issues. If you don't believe me, the next time you're at a conference just ask some of your colleagues that own service companies what their number one problem is and I guarantee that 90% of them will say something that has to do with employees. The fact is that these owners and managers can play the part and they have the title, but almost everyone who comes in contact with their companies ends up having a negative experience.

For the owner and managers, their business is a place that they can't stand because everything becomes a distraction from doing excellent technical work. They have all of these other "inconvenient" responsibilities like dealing with employee issues, training, banking, marketing and a nearly endless list of other business activities.

Things are no better for the front line employees of the technician-owned service company. For the good employees, it's just a job until something better comes along. These employees are not clear on what to do, and even if they are, how they're doing on the job is rarely communicated. The good employees see their peers get away with murder with no accountability because the owner and managers simply don't know what's going on. They're too busy doing the technical work.

The end result is that technician-owned and managed service companies simply don't work. The culture at these companies is toxic and each day flows like a bad episode of Jerry Springer. Each day, both the front line and the managers come in to numb the pain once again without giving any thought to resolving the real problems of the business. It's painful for everyone involved.

The real problem is that most of these technician owners and managers never stop to consider what a customer of their business experiences. These owners and managers accept a false assumption: if the technical work they perform is superior to other companies, then the customer will see and appreciate them as a business. Nothing could be further from the truth.

Before we get into the framework, there is something that you need to know about me and the purpose of this book.

I REALLY COULDN'T CARE LESS

Years ago, when I started my service company, I didn't have a clue as to what I was doing. I didn't know how to manage people, I didn't know how to read a P&L, and I certainly didn't know how to build a service company. I had built a successful software consulting company before but I didn't have employees nor was I attempting to build a company larger than just myself.

I knew then that I needed to learn more about managing and leading people because, let's face it, if you own or manage a service company, what you really do is lead and manage people.

Fortunately for me, at that time I knew what was missing, and any time I wasn't working in the business I spent reading popular management and business books. Most of these books espoused the idea that if I would just be nice and inspire people, then they in turn would give me their best. All I had to do as an owner and leader was dream, believe, and inspire others, and the rest of the business would take care of itself.

At the time, I didn't realize that most of these books were written by consultants and professors who hadn't ever actually started and grown a service company themselves. It didn't take long for me to discover that most of the books and the ideas that they promoted were total and complete garbage. These books are very heavy on ideas that may make you feel all warm and fuzzy inside, but they're very light on the ideas that make a real company work, like account-ability, checklists, systems, and hard work.

Well, in this book we're going to go light on the feelings and go heavy on the pragmatics of building a great company. It's a good thing that I don't make my living writing books, because I am going to share with you the real truth behind what it takes to build a phenomenal company. I'm a business owner and entrepreneur, first and foremost, and that's how I earn my living. I couldn't care less about feelings or book sales or how many people agree with me. So when I say that I really couldn't care less, I really mean that. If that bothers you or if you're offended by that then you probably should put this book down and go find another book, perhaps on self-esteem. It's not that I don't want to see others succeed or that I'm calloused and indifferent to others. It's the fact that I know what works and I know what doesn't and I'm indifferent as to whether you agree or not, because I'm not trying to sell you anything.

The system that I'm about to share with you works. I've seen it work in my own businesses and I've seen it work in other businesses, service sectors and markets. I've seen this system work in service companies that range from medical services to lavatory services. It's time-tested and proven. Time and time again this system, if followed, has built a great company that customers love and where employees love to work.

I DECIDED TO WRITE THIS BOOK FOR TWO PRIMARY REASONS:

The first reason is that I want to give anyone who decides to join my team, especially leaders, a gift that I never had: a basic framework on how to build a great life, a great department, a great division, and ultimately a great company. I want everyone on my team to know and deeply understand why we do things the way that we do them, and how to approach building and sustaining a phenomenal company.

The second reason is that oftentimes other business owners visit one of my companies and inevitably asks how I grew them and how they can replicate my success. This book will serve as a starting point to get out of the theoretical and into the practical, with simple steps to achieve the same results I did.

CHAPTER SUMMARY & ACTION CHECKLIST

- There are two parts to a problem: The root cause and the outward symptoms.
- Treating the symptoms will bring temporary relief, but, left without treatment, the cause will only fester and get worse.
- Being a service technician and running a service business are two different skill sets.
- Owning or managing a service business requires removing oneself from the technical work and focusing on the organization as a whole.
- This framework is what you make of it. You have to put the work into it to get the best results out of it.
- Go to coalmarch.com/build to download the resources for this chapter and all chapters to follow.

"Your reputation and integrity are everything. Follow through on what you say you're going to do. Your credibility can only be built over time, and it is built from the history of your words and actions."

- Maria Razumich-Zec

Chapter 2

The Technician's Illusion

In July of 2010, Elmendorf Air Force Base in Anchorage, Alaska was abuzz with activity as it prepared to host its world famous annual Arctic Thunder Air Show. Each year, pilots and aircraft from all over the world descend on Alaska to participate in this premier world event. For the pilot community, the Arctic Thunder Air Show is one of the most sought-after air shows to participate in. It features almost every aircraft in the U.S. Air Force's inventory along with the most famous and accomplished acrobatic and stunt pilots from all over the world.

The crowning event of the 2010 air show was the aerial display from all of the aircraft assigned to the 176th Alaska Air National Guard Wing in Anchorage. As the largest and most complex wings in the Air National Guard, supporting airlift, search and rescue, air defense, and special operations, the 176th had the most diverse and largest inventory of transport aircraft and search and rescue helicopters.

The crown jewel of the 176th aircraft inventory and the focus of the finale aerial display was the C-17 Globemaster, the most accomplished and technologically capable air transport aircraft in the U.S. Air Force history. Three years earlier, the 176th added this aircraft to inventory on base and the C-17 was a favorite to those that lived on base and to the locals who lived in the Anchorage area.

On the evening of July 28th 2010, three days before the airshow was set to start, Sitka 43, a freshly cleaned and painted C-17, was cleared to taxi across a crowded ramp of airshow aircraft to runway 06 for takeoff.

Major Freyholtz was by a long shot the most highly respected and seasoned C-17 pilot in the 176th. With more than 3500 flying hours under his belt, 608 of which were combat hours, Freyholtz was the first C-17 pilot instructor and flight examiner for the wing. He was also the 176th's first Air Show Demonstration pilot for the C-17. He even served a tour with the elite United States Air Force Thunderbirds the previous year, demonstrating the C-17's capabilities in air shows all over the world.

Upon reaching the runway 06, Sitka 43 was cleared for takeoff. Freyholtz took the runway and immediately began the air show flight demonstration that he'd developed over the previous year while flying with the Thunderbirds. As the aircraft approached the required flight speed, Major Freyholtz initiated an aggressive 40 degree steep climb.

Within the first 10 seconds of the flight, Major Freyholtz made two major errors. His first error was not allowing the aircraft's airspeed to come within 33 knots of the USAF's mandatory minimum for the C-17. The second was leveling off at 850 feet above the ground; barely half the minimum altitude required for the next maneuver in his air show profile.

Once he leveled off, Freyholtz banked left by more than 60 degrees, rapidly repositioning the C-17 for a high-speed pass over the runway.

Upon completing the left turn, Freyholtz then banked the aircraft right by more than 60 degrees, rather than the USAF's prescribed, 45 degree bank limit. In so doing, Freyholtz loaded the aircraft with 2.4g while the C-17 was traveling at more than 6 knots below the stall speed. Stall speed is the speed at which the aircraft can no longer maintain flight. That is to say, if you stall an aircraft in flight, the aircraft ceases to fly and becomes nothing more than a large paperweight.

Freyholtz's slow speed coupled with his aggressive 60 degree bank triggered an automatic stall warning system on the C-17 that literally shook the control stick and caused the word "stall" to be repeated over the intercom multiple times.

Freyholtz initially disregarded the warning system as he believed it was inaccurate during such a maneuver. Ignoring this warning system was the final and most critical mistake Freyholtz made in the flight.

Already dangerously low, the aircraft passed into a deep stall while the safety observer, Malone, swiftly repeated this phrase three times: "Watch your bank, watch your bank, watch your bank." Freyholtz, intent on completing the turn, reversed his stick pressure, while at the same time applying left rudder, which made the stall even worse. Just seconds later, a perfectly functioning C-17 performing a routine airshow practice flight crashed into a small field just outside the base, killing all four crew members on board.

QUESTIONS AND LESSONS

After the fatal crash, the Air Force assembled an accident investigation team to determine exactly how the highly capable C-17 aircraft with a highly skilled and seasoned pilot at its controls crashed only 50 seconds into flight on a routine air show practice profile.

Why would Major Freyholtz fly the airplane too slow? Why did he overbank the aircraft outside operating limitations? Why did he level off at only half the altitude required for the maneuver? Why did he ignore the clear signs that he was about to stall the airplane?

Ultimately, the accident investigation team determined that pilot error was the primary cause of the crash. The board concluded that Major Freyholtz, while a gifted and highly experienced pilot, ignored simple and basic flying rules and procedures. The accident board was astonished at how Major Freyholtz and his crew completely disregarded procedures and operating boundaries that even much less experienced student pilots would never dare to cross.

The lesson I want you to take home from this crash is that no matter how good you are, or how good you think you are, there must always be a healthy respect for the basics in any endeavor. Basics such as flying at a safe airspeed, at a safe altitude, and following basic procedures that are taught to pilots on the very first day of pilot training. While there are thousands upon thousands of other details that you must know as a pilot, following and adhering to the basics is what keeps you alive.

Unfortunately, choosing to ignore simple but basic rules in any endeavor, whether it's flying airplanes or operating a business, can and will hurt you, and in some cases may even be fatal.

INTEGRITY - THE MOST BASIC OF THE BASICS

Would you consider integrity as a "basic" in the realm of business?

Do you consider your company to be a company of integrity?

If so, why do you believe that it is?

If not, why do you think that is?

What exactly do you think the word integrity means?

If there ever was a word in the business world that is completely misunderstood and totally misused, it has be the word integrity. Oftentimes when people speak of integrity, either personally or in a business setting, they are referring to its ethical definition:

Integrity (Ethics Definition) - The honesty and truthfulness or accuracy of one's actions.

While this definition is accurate and completely consistent with personal integrity, it isn't the complete definition.

The word integrity evolved from the Latin adjective integer, meaning whole or complete. In a "non-ethical" context, the full definition of integrity is:

Integrity (full definition) - Being in a state of "wholeness" in which actions reflect qualities such as honesty and consistency of character.

In pop business culture, many gurus, owners, and well-meaning managers will brag about and extol the integrity of their organizations or the integrity of their employees. These owners and managers mistakenly believe that because they are honest with their employees and honest with their customers, that by default, they own and operate a company of integrity. That is to say, to them, they already have the "basics" of integrity nailed into their business.

For most service companies, nothing could be further from the truth.

Years ago when I was accepted into pilot training, my wife and I were already well on our way to establishing a family. We'd bought our first home and Emily was pregnant with our first child. Pilot training required us to move around the country for the next three years and the plan was for my wife and little one to join me.

Knowing that I'd eventually return to the Raleigh area, I decided not to sell our house, but instead rent it out while we were away. In order to do this, I'd have to set up services to maintain our home in our absence.

Not knowing where to start, I emailed my neighbors for recommendations. For lawn maintenance, several neighbors highly recommended Dave, a one-man lawn maintenance company. My neighbors gave him glowing recommendations like "Dave does a wonderful job" and "Dave does a better job than I do." Many of the recommendations had back-sided warnings attached to them as well, which I didn't pay much attention to at the time, but I should have. They gave Dave (and Dave's company) a great recommendation, but would end with a slightly negative comment like "... but he is very busy", or ".... but you will need to call him a lot."

I decided to give Dave a shot at my lawn for 6 months prior to us moving so that I could make sure that he was the right person for the job.

As it turned out, my neighbors were correct. When Dave mowed my lawn the first time, my lawn looked like a lawn you would see on the cover of a golf magazine. He did a spectacular job by every measure. Although I'm a little embarrassed to admit it, Dave really did a much better job than I ever did.

The next week, Dave showed up and did the same spectacular work that he'd performed the previous week. On the third week, Dave didn't make it to our place on Wednesday due to some "unforeseen circumstances," but he came on Thursday instead. "No worries; those things happen," I thought. On the fourth week, he didn't show up until Friday, again due to "unforeseen circumstances." The week after that, Dave didn't show at all. If you guessed that it was due to unforeseen circumstances, you're right. And so it went for three months with Dave as my lawn maintenance provider. Each week, "unforeseen circumstances" seemed to rule the service.

Some weeks Dave would come on Monday, and other weeks Dave would come on Friday. There were weeks when Dave would simply not show up at all. When he didn't show, I'd call him and leave messages, but he never returned my calls. In fact, after the first mowing I never got another phone call from Dave. I found it quite interesting how, before our agreement, he always seemed available to take my calls. But now, nothing.

Each time Dave would arrive at my home to mow the lawn he followed the same routine:

1. Dave would apologize profusely about not coming out earlier.
2. Dave would have some story as to why he could not call me back. Phone broke, voicemail down, not getting messages. None of these were problems before our agreement.
3. Dave would explain the reasons why he couldn't come out on the agreed upon day of the week to maintain the lawn. (After two months of inconsistent days, I don't believe he even knew what day he was supposed to come to my home to mow the lawn.)

4. Dave would mow the lawn and tell me that we should be "good to go" moving forward. I don't think that he was intentionally misleading me. I think he honestly believed that.

Despite Dave's honesty and the quality of his work, I ultimately ended up firing him. There was nothing more frustrating for me as a customer than the inconsistency of his service and his lack of communication. Some weeks my lawn looked like the Serengeti and on other weeks it looked like a course on the PGA tour. Then there was the communication issue. I could never get in touch with Dave to figure out what was going on, so I just stopped trying.

The reality is that most service companies, especially home service companies, have zero integrity. That's not to say these are dishonest companies with immoral employees, because most companies certainly are not.

What I am saying is that at the end of the day, most home service companies lack basic integrity. That is, these companies are honest, but they completely miss the whole and consistent parts of the integrity definition.

RELIABILITY - THE CORNERSTONE OF INTEGRITY

Recently a research team conducted a large study of recurring services across multiple industries with the goal of trying to determine exactly why customers cancel services (personal services, home services or software services).

The results of the research were not surprising. The main finding of the research determined that there are 5 primary reasons that customers leave service companies. These are:

- 1% die
- 3% move
- 14% switch to a competitor
- 14% are dissatisfied with the service
- 68% leave due to poor attitude or indifference

Many technician owned and operated companies falsely believe that if they provide a great service, their customers will see, understand, and appreciate the quality of the work while at the same time overlook "little" things that technicians are generally not good at, like communication and consistency.

This research, and my own experience, clearly indicates otherwise. Most customers already expect you to be an expert in the service that you provide and in reality they look to other indicators of your service for quality.

These other indicators have absolutely nothing to do with service and are typically things that your customer can see and understand.

Think about it. If you are a medical provider, do you expect your patients to understand exactly how a specific body system works? Do you believe that when you're done diagnosing them that they're going to completely understand the diagnosis?

Imagine you own an auto repair facility. Do you expect the customer to completely understand the coolant system of their car and how dependant the other systems of the vehicle are on that system? If you perform a repair do you believe that the customer will understand and see the quality of it?

The fact is, and research shows, that customers rarely use the service itself as an indicator of quality and value.

In their landmark research of service quality perceptions, Dr. Valerie Zeithaml, Dr. A. Parasuraman and Dr. Leonard Berry of the University of North Carolina Kenan-Flagler business school discovered that what customers perceive as "value" actually has nothing to do with service at all.

These researchers uncovered the 5 elements that truly determine customer perception of quality that ultimately leads to customer loyalty. These are:

1. **Tangibles.** Appearance of physical facilities, equipment, personnel, and communication materials.

2. **Reliability.** Ability to perform the promised service dependably and accurately.

3. **Responsiveness.** Willingness to help customers and provide prompt service.

4. **Assurance.** Knowledge and courtesy of employees and their ability to convey trust and confidence.

5. **Empathy.** Caring, individualized attention the firm provides its customers.

While not all elements were given equal weight, reliability was the highest of all five indicators by a factor of two.

THE TECHNICIAN'S ILLUSION

Most technician owned and operated companies completely miss the fact that most customers expect the service to be effective and to be good. This illusion is as dangerous as it is alarming.

Think about it. Do you believe that the airshow crowds that Major Freyholtz performed for prior to his accident would have been able to tell the difference in climbing at the minimum C-17 speed or 33 knots below the minimum climb speed? Would the crowd have thought any less of the C-17 capabilities if the stunt had been performed 500 feet higher? Would a spectator really be able to tell the difference between a 45 degree turn and a dangerous 60 degree one?

Therein lies the problem with most technicians turned owner or manager. Just like Major Freyholtz, in an effort to give the best possible service, they completely and totally ignore the basics of what really satisfies their customers. Don't mistake what I'm saying. I'm neither encouraging nor advocating that you provide crappy service that's ineffective or inadequate.

What I am saying is that your company must be the whole package. That is, your company must have real integrity, which means consistently providing great service and paying attention to all the other factors that your customers care about, like great communication.

Most technicians-turned-business-owners and managers struggle with this concept because the tech work is something that they love to do and it's something that they're fully invested in. Most would rather not be bothered by customers who expect them to focus on seemingly less important things such as great communication or following through on commitments. Almost all of these technicians have a flawed assumption: that customers give more weight to the service than to other less important factors, such as showing up on time or returning a phone call.

If you get nothing else from this chapter, understand this: Just as airspeed and altitude are the basic critical elements that keep an aircraft safe while flying, complete integrity and reliability in your service are the critical elements that will attract and retain customers for your company over the long term.

A technician owned and managed company cannot keep customers or employees over the long term because they have no real integrity. Technician owned and managed companies are the worst companies to purchase service from and they're the worst companies to work for. These technician owners and managers would rather focus on the technical aspects of their service instead of focusing on what will truly satisfy customers and retain employees.

But there is a better way. It is possible to build a company that both customers and employees love. A company that grows year after year and is highly profitable. That is what the Build™ platform is all about, building a phenomenal company based on total integrity.

CHAPTER SUMMARY & ACTION CHECKLIST

- A business with integrity acts with honesty and consistency of character.
- Doing good technical work is not enough. A service business must consider what is most important to its customers – reliability, thoughtfulness, empathy, etc. – and provide consistent results across the board.
- Fostering an environment with integrity is the foundation for growing a better business.
- Go to coalmarch.com/build to download the resources for this chapter

"A bad system
will beat a good
person every
time."

- W. Edwards Deming

Chapter 3

Adrenaline Doesn't Belong in Your Business

Between operating a couple of businesses and raising four small children at home, I rarely, if ever, have time to sit down and watch a television program. When other adults start talking about the plot of a sitcom or the latest series on Netflix, I'm typically the weird guy that stares at the ceiling or quickly changes the conversation because I simply can't relate. At this point in my life there's simply too much to do and not enough time to get it all done.

Frankly, the only time I watch at all is with my little ones, so it should be no surprise that most of what I've seen over the last 10 years has been animated Disney films.

If you've ever seen a Disney movie, or any children's movie for that matter, you've essentially seen them all. That is to say they all have the same basic plot. While it's usually the villain that steals the spotlight, these movies always have a great hero. Not necessarily an unbeatable, incredible, awesome hero, but some kind of relatable figure with generous amounts of goodwill and personality.

The plot typically follows the following sequence:

1. There's a person, a hero, who despite some flaws, we sympathize with and cheer on.
2. The hero must overcome some really big obstacle (physical or mental).
3. There's a villain who tries to stop the hero.
4. Drama unfolds as the hero overcomes the obstacles.
5. Despite the incredible odds and coming close to defeat, the hero pulls off the unthinkable and saves the day.

This one basic plot accounts for billions of dollars of movie ticket sales and it has application in both animated and non-animated movies. Think about it. James Bond can get shot at over a 1,000 times in a movie and every single shot misses, leaving him unscathed. However, when Bond shoots, each and every shot is right on target, and he takes down the villain.

We all love to watch heroes, and experience a little drama. We all love the idea of a superhuman person who, like us, has struggles but somehow always finds a way to overcome their challenges and ultimately win. These heroes not only live a life that most of us will never experience, they're also able to pull off feats that mere mortals like us would not even attempt.

I don't have a beef with heroes. I love them just the same as you do. Heroes are entertaining and save the day. Heroes make great movies and keep the universe in balance by masterfully defeating villain after villain.

THE SYSTEMS ENGINEER

Imagine for a moment that you decide to treat your significant other with a night out on the town. You carefully plan how the evening will go down. First, you'll surprise him or her with a small gift, then you surprise them with an itinerary that details just how the two of you will spend the evening together.

First stop of the evening is dinner. You painstakingly took the time to pick the nicest restaurant in town. You checked and even made sure that the chef could and would make the favorite dish that your significant other loves. Following dinner, you plan a nice walk, so the two of you can have some laughs and reconnect. Finally the evening will end with a movie at the finest theater in town, followed by activities that are beyond the scope of this book.

As you begin the evening, everything's going as planned. Your significant other could not be more appreciative of the small thoughtful gift that you gave them and is excited about the evening to come. The restaurant is perfect. The manager takes special care to seat you both near a window where the view is absolutely breathtaking. Your waiter is on point all evening and the food tastes like it was cooked by Gordon Ramsay of Hell's Kitchen himself. Your walk after dinner is delightful. As you stroll through the gardens of the park, the connection and spark that attracted you to each other is now as strong as ever. No doubt this evening is turning out to be better than you'd ever imagined.

The feeling of connection gets only stronger as you take your seats in the movie theater. Holding hands you both anticipate a wonderful movie followed by some "alone time" to round out this perfect date night.

As the movie begins, you realize something is amiss. The opening scene features a geeky guy sitting in front of a large computer. After about 2 minutes of this scene, you realize that the movie is about the day in the life of an engineer. The first scene of the movie is nothing more than the engineer viewing business operation performance reports. The next scene is even worse than the first, as it features a boring meeting in which the engineer discusses how to improve the performance of the service delivery system. And just when you think the movie couldn't get any worse, in a moment full of fabricated drama, the engineer is shown at his desk drawing a flowchart of modifications to improve the service delivery system.

Aghast that such a movie would ever be produced, you and your significant other walk out of the theater. The wonderful night and feeling that you had is now gone. The movie of the systems engineer improving his service delivery system completely decimated the mood that you and your significant other had earlier in the evening. You vow to never, I do mean never, ever pay to go and see another movie that stars an engineer. Your relationship just can't handle another buzzkill like that.

THE HERO OR THE SYSTEMS ENGINEER?

No doubt about it, the systems engineer is clearly not cut out for Hollywood. If Hollywood built its entertainment model based on the day in the life of an engineer, most producers would be on a street corner with a hat collecting change. What suspense is there in not saving the day? What's exciting about systems and designing processes? What drama can be pulled from reviewing performance reports and then making adjustments?

The fact is that most engineers and the job of engineering is almost totally and completely void of any drama whatsoever. Typically, the systems engineer is a dull, no-frills person and the job of engineering is quite frankly boring to watch. There's nothing sexy about the engineer or an engineering job itself. As an engineer, there are no lives to save, no drama to create and no insurmountable situation that must be dealt with right now.

The fact is, the systems engineer detests having to save the day. The engineer is perfectly happy with a dull normal day with the systems operating as they should.

In contrast, the hero is a total and complete adrenaline junkie. Day in and day out, the hero lives a life full of drama and excitement. Each day the hero faces challenges that only he can overcome. Everyone loves the hero. The hero can make things happen. The hero knows how to pull the unthinkable off. The hero can solve problems that other mere mortals would never dream they could resolve.

For a moment, think about your company. Wouldn't it be great to have a staff of heroes that can make things happen? Would it not make your company one of the best, most competitive companies in your market if your team constantly overcame insurmountable odds to win each and every time? Doesn't it make sense that a team of heroes can and will beat any other team in your market and in your industry?

Many years ago, an Air Force Reserve unit near my home had a very competitive military pilot position become available. Normally these positions were reserved for and awarded to highly experienced and seasoned pilots transitioning from active duty. Despite the odds of me actually getting selected, I applied and surprisingly was offered the slot. Somehow I'd convinced the unit that I was the right person for the pilot slot even though I had zero flying experience.

I still remember the day that I was notified that I'd been selected. I was so excited that I decided I would visit the unit to meet my new commander and the other pilots in the unit. My new commander couldn't have been kinder. He spent the entire afternoon walking me through what to expect for the next three years of my life and introduced me to all the pilots and staff in the squadron. At the end of the tour, he introduced me to his team of administrative assistants. As he introduced me to each one, he took some extra time to introduce me to Susan. According to my new commander, Susan was a rockstar in the squadron. She could make things happen and she was awesome at her job. When a crisis arose, Susan was the person that my commander trusted to resolve the crisis and to get things done.

In the military absolutely nothing happens without orders. You need orders to coordinate a move, you need orders to get paid, you need orders for medical and dental services and the list goes on and on. In short, before I could transition to the unit and eventually on to pilot training, I needed orders. As it turned out, to my delight, Susan "the rockstar" was the person who handled orders for the unit.

At the end of my visit with the commander, he said in passing "Just let Susan know that you need the orders and she'll get you all taken care of." As instructed, before I left the base I "let Susan know" that I needed orders. She congratulated me and said "No problem, I'll get your orders all done by the end of the week. Monday at the latest."

That Monday came and I called. No orders yet. There was an emergency at the squadron and Susan needed to step in to handle the situation. Susan assured me that the orders would get done this week and to contact her the following Monday. When I followed up the next Monday there'd been yet another emergency that week and Susan was once again unable to process the orders. No worries she said. "Just a lot happening right now and a couple of emergencies I needed to handle. Give me another week and I'll get you all squared away."

Six months later, and two weeks before I was scheduled to depart for training, I was getting the same story. Exasperated, I drove to the base and literally went and sat in Susan's empty office to wait for her. Finding me in her office upon her arrival, Susan was unimpressed by my presence. Highly frustrated, I laid on the sarcasm as I reviewed how for the last six months I'd attempted to get my orders but each week "emergencies" seemed to take priority over them. I also explained how I only had a week now to prepare all of the necessary items for the transition.

As I was laying on the sarcasm, my commander strolled into the office and Susan changed her demeanor immediately. She told the commander about the urgent need for me to get orders (news flash) and that she'd drop everything and get them done that very morning. Ladies and gentlemen, we have a crisis and this calls for a hero. And being the hero, Susan didn't let me down. In just one hour, I had orders in my hands to make my transition to training.

Once she finished the orders, the commander came into her office and personally thanked her "heroic effort" in this small drama. Susan even looked to me to offer praise for what she'd just accomplished.

I couldn't offer her any praise. How could I? I was beside myself. I'd been waiting on these orders for over six months. I had to physically drive to her office to get them. It only took her one hour to process them. Instead of having six months to transition out, I had less than two weeks because of her procrastination. How was that something to be celebrated or praised? In my mind, I couldn't help but wonder how in six months time she didn't have one hour to process my orders?

While I was not a "customer" in the traditional sense of the word, I can tell you that the customer experience was nothing short of "major suckage". What could have been simply handled in an hour without any drama or fanfare was instead pushed into a modern day blockbuster drama in which Susan, the hero, yet again saved the day.

The only problem with Susan being the hero of this drama was that other people and agencies now had their own minor dramas to accommodate heroic Susan's procrastination. Think about it. Now instead of having six months to coordinate a move, the movers now had less than two weeks. Instead of base housing having six months to prepare a home for my family with a small child, they now had less than two weeks. Instead of finance having six months to get me into the pay system, they had less than two weeks. While Susan's actions created the perception that she was doing a great job and saving the day, the fact is that she was making everyone's day (and job) much worse than it needed to be.

WHAT THE SYSTEMS ENGINEER KNOWS THAT THE HERO DOESN'T

While heroes sell movies and make great entertainment, they've no place in your business. Heroes spend all of their time resolving issues but never any time solving the problems that created those issues.

When a problem arises or a "situation" comes up, the hero immediately springs into action. The hero knows what to do, when to do it and how to get things done. The hero can pull off a feat that other employees simply will not or cannot do. When the hero saves the day, peers are amazed, management is amazed, in fact, everyone is amazed. That is, everyone with the exception of the systems engineer.

You see, the systems engineer doesn't view saving the day as something to be celebrated at all. In reality, the systems engineer sees having to save the day as a failure. While everyone else is celebrating and trading fist bumps, the systems engineer is thinking differently. The systems engineer is wondering what went wrong that required a hero's effort to resolve.

A hero would rather save the day, and have an ego boost in the process, rather than go through the arduous process of determining the problem that created the issue in the first place. Lets face it, if the problem is solved and the issue never comes up again then the hero cannot save the day – and where's the adrenaline rush in that?

The systems engineer wants the exact opposite of the hero. The systems engineer knows that when things are going smoothly, the likelihood of things getting done on time and properly go up exponentially. The systems engineer gets his ego boost by things being boring, predictable and normal, rather than exciting, unpredictable, and dramatic. The systems engineer is more interested in preventing dramas and heroic scenarios before they begin to erupt. Dramas and heroics point to a system failure. The hero's need for drama is validation that something's not right in your business.

The systems engineer knows people. The systems engineer knows that people are inconsistent, emotional, irrational and oftentimes unreliable. The systems engineer knows that while the hero pulled through this time and won, in the long term such victories are rare.

In real life, heroes seldom exist. In situations where a hero is needed, defeats are much more common than victories. The systems engineer knows that it's much easier to design and develop a good system that works than it is to find, train, and motivate hero after hero for the business.

BUILD YOUR BUSINESS, DON'T SAVE IT

Sadly, there is a glut of owners and managers who, just like Susan, don't get this one simple concept:

As an owner or manager, your job is to build your business, not save it.

That is to say, your job is to be a systems engineer, not a hero.

Many owners and managers are totally and completely confused about their role and responsibilities at their company. Many believe that their role is to be good at reacting to problems and to be the best at the technical work of the business – a hero. They go about their day resolving one problem after the next. Perfectly happy doing the technical work and being the go-to person to get things done. It feels great. They feel accomplished and people depend on them.

What these owners and managers fail to see is that while they're off saving the day, the underlying causes that created the issues initially are never really being addressed. They can't be. Who has time for that? There are so many crises to solve! Who has time to sit down and think about why the same problems keep happening and why a hero's effort is required day in and day out to operate the business? Who has time to work on the business? In their mind, there is not enough time to simply get the regular work done.

Owners and managers that work in their business face the same problems year after year. Owners and managers that work in their business never see their company progress. Sales are flat, profit is flat, and the company operates the same today as it did five years ago. Owners and managers that work in their business see their employees check their brains at the door because they're so exhausted. Owners and managers that work in their business fight the same battles, day after day, year after year, decade after decade. They're nothing more than fabricated heroes that either don't understand what they should be doing or have the need to be psychologically needed. That is, they need to be a hero.

Conversely, owners and managers that work on their businesses never have the same year twice. While some businesses have the same year 30 times, these businesses have 30 years of experience. That's because these owners and managers understand that their role is that of a systems engineer. They look at the business as one giant system and just as a dutiful engineer would, they work to improve the system each and every day. When a problem arises, instead of craving the rush of adrenaline to save the day, these owners and managers dissect the situation, they look beyond the immediate issue and they identify the real problem. These owners and managers understand that the technical work is to be done by technicians, and systems development is to be done by them.

Responsible parents understand that in order to raise happy, self-reliant and resilient children they must avoid the temptation of saving and rescuing their children and instead focus on teaching them how to face and overcome challenges themselves. Likewise owners and managers who build strong, profitable companies understand that, like responsible parents, their role is not to save their companies but to build the business and people systems that can produce a thriving company without them. Research study after research study shows that companies with strong systems hands down consistently outperform hero companies in value, scalability, customer experience, and ultimately, profitability.

CHAPTER SUMMARY & ACTION CHECKLIST

- Heroes may be flashy and exciting, but in business, always saving the day means something is always wrong.
- A healthy business is run by systems engineers, not heroes. They build systems that work and find their thrill in watching them succeed. Be a systems engineer.
- Get out of the technical work. As an owner or manager, your job is to maintain the systems of your company. Ignoring the big picture hurts your company and your team.
- Functioning business systems deliver better value, growth opportunity, customer experience, and profitability.
- Go to coalmarch.com/build to download the resources for this chapter

"Wise men learn more from fools than fools from the wise."

- Cato the Elder

Chapter 4

A Company or a System?

On the morning of February 20th 1995, retired heavy equipment operator Willie King checked into the University Community Hospital in Tampa, Florida. For years, Willie struggled with and suffered from the effects of diabetes, and now the disease was attacking both of his legs and feet. Diabetes had left Willie with ulcers on both feet and an inability to feel them due to nerve damage. One of the ulcers on Willie's right foot had become infected, but with a compromised immune system, Willie's body was unable to fight the infection.

Willie was left with a choice. He could continue to live in extreme pain as the infection spread through his body or he could have a life-altering surgery in which his lower right leg would be amputated. As Willie considered his options his doctors assured him that while amputation was a serious procedure, it was also a common one, with minimal risks for someone in his condition.

Reluctantly, Willie made the decision to move forward with the life-altering surgery and decided to schedule it as soon as possible.

The following Monday morning, just after the surgery, Willie thought for a moment that maybe the medication used to sedate him was having a dramatic effect. To Willie's complete and total surprise, his right leg hadn't been amputated during the surgery, but his left leg had. Describing the event in a later press conference, Willie exclaimed, "when I came to and discovered I lost my good one, it was a shock, a real shock. I told him: "Doctor, that's the wrong leg."

After (wisely) choosing another hospital to perform the correct amputation, Willie settled out of court for an undisclosed sum, and both University Hospital and the surgeon were slapped with severe fines. The whole ordeal remains one of the most publicized cases of medical malpractice in history.

An investigation into the incident revealed four critical mistakes that led to the medical malpractice award.

The first mistake occurred days before the procedure, when the operating room scheduler accidentally identified the left leg for amputation instead of the right.

The second mistake occurred on the morning of the procedure, when instead of checking patient consent forms and procedure authorization forms, the operating staff assumed that the schedule was correct and listed the left leg on the operating chalkboard.

The third mistake occurred when, assuming the chalkboard was correct, the operating room nurse prepped Willie's left leg for amputation. While it may seem unfathomable that a nurse could do this, you have to keep in mind that both of Willie's legs had infected ulcers. It was only in WIllie's right leg that the infection had progressed to the point of requiring amputation.

The fourth mistake occurred when the operating staff sedated Willie without actually speaking with him about the procedure. It's customary, before any surgical procedure, for the surgeon to actually speak to the patient to confirm the procedure that they're about to perform. The operating room staff routinely ignored this formality as they felt having to wait for the patient to be sedated after the surgeon arrived was a waste of time.

With the schedule indicating the left leg to be amputated, along with the operating chalkboard displaying the left leg, along with the left leg being prepped for amputation, along with no visual cues that the left leg was not a good candidate for amputation, the stage was set for the surgeon to amputate the wrong leg.

QUESTIONS TO CONSIDER

When a person visits the doctor's office or the emergency room, they should receive the medical care that they need. Unfortunately, the standard of this medical care varies widely from hospital to hospital. In the most extreme incidences, the very hands that are supposed to be helping a patient can ultimately become the cause of their death.

While Willie King's case and the resulting medical malpractice is dramatic and somewhat unbelievable, it's surprisingly predictable and expected at some hospitals. Cases of heart surgery being performed on the wrong patient, wrong arteries being bypassed and even medical tools being left inside of patients is more common than you think, even today.

As you consider the case of Willie King, there are some basic questions worth asking:

1. How could a professional hospital that performs thousands of procedures a year overlook such a basic and critical detail?
2. How did a simple mistake like listing the wrong leg in the scheduling software end up with the wrong leg actually being amputated?
3. What do you think the culture was like at the hospital?
4. Do you think that the hospital could have benefited from a simple checklist prior to the procedure that

confirmed everything before the surgeon whipped out a knife and started cutting on the patient?

5. Would you like to have surgery at this hospital? This was the only mistake made out of thousands of procedures; does that matter to you?

YOUR COMPANY IS A SYSTEM

All of these questions have far-reaching and complex answers. In the final analysis, instead of improving the quality of Willie's life, the hospital made his life worse not better. By every measure, the University Community Hospital failed Willie King, or did it?

In her excellent book, Thinking in Systems, Donella Meadows defines a system as "a set of connected things or parts forming a complex whole, in particular". Expanding on this definition, it means that almost everything you do on a day-to-day basis is really nothing more than a system.

Scheduling surgery is a system. Recording operations to be performed in an operating room is a system. Preparing a limb for amputation is a system, and all of these systems are subsystems of an amputation system. If you expand that out even further, performing surgeries is a system, billing insurance companies is a system, operating a 24-hour emergency room is a system and relocating patients between rooms is a system. These systems are really nothing more than subsystems of the hospital operational systems.

Revisiting the case of Willie King, it wasn't the hospital that failed him, it was the lack of systems and procedures.

If you only take one idea from this chapter, remember this:

A company is nothing more than a system made up of several sub-systems.

Some may argue that in the case of University Community Hospital there were systems and procedures in place to prevent such an error. However, using the definition of a system, validating that employees follow procedures and holding them accountable for operating the systems is a system as well.

WHAT EXACTLY IS A GREAT COMPANY?

At the risk of sounding like the Dalai Lama or Socrates, for a moment I want you to consider one essential question - the answer to which, if you can articulate it clearly, will be a guide for your company and your business career. The question is simply this:

What exactly is a phenomenal company?

As simple and as straightforward as this question sounds, the answer is more elusive than you might think. In fact, I bet if you sat in a room full of company owners and managers and asked this simple question you'd get at least 20 different answers. That's because we all have different values and we all have different ideas of what constitutes a great company.

Every service company, simple or complex, large or small, has four primary stakeholders. These are: customers, employees, vendors, and owners.

It's not my place to tell you what you should value or how you should define a great company; however, I can tell you that no company can achieve lasting greatness without a system that balances the needs of all stakeholders over the long term.

The reason that most business owners and managers struggle and never reach their potential is that they fail to view their businesses as one giant system designed to satisfy the needs of all of the stakeholders. Instead, these owners and managers see their businesses defined in arbitrary ideas that focus on one stakeholder at the exclusion of the other three.

For example, many business owners and managers believe that if they are a larger company with more revenue and higher profits than most of their industry peers, that alone will define them as a great company.

To these owners and managers I ask: When was the last time you shopped at Walmart?

Walmart earns billions of dollars of revenue and billions of dollars of profit, yet most customers who shop there hate the place. Long lines, rude employees and damaged product are the norm. Most employees who work at Walmart hate the place. If you don't believe that, just observe Walmart employees next time you shop in one of their stores. Walmart is also notorious for pressuring and squeezing its vendors into selling at a loss so that Walmart can offer competitive prices while preserving its own profit. Would you consider this company great? You might, but their customers, employees, and vendors wouldn't agree.

Other owners and managers believe that a great company is one that offers the highest wages and best benefits. The logic, in this case, is that a company is great because it takes care of its employees.

To these owners and managers, I ask: Do you want to be like General Motors?

In 2009, General Motors (GM) filed for Chapter 11 bankruptcy following the stock market meltdown due to the mortgage industry crisis. For decades, GM had provided high-paying jobs to its employees along with generous pension and retirement packages. Having made unrealistic promises to its employees, GM found itself losing marketshare to companies that were producing vehicles at a fraction of the cost because these companies did not bear the burden of a bloated compensation and retirement system.

After years of providing high paying jobs complete with all of the perks, GM simply could not compete with other companies that paid their employees market-appropriate salaries. This ultimately led to GM filing Chapter 11 and being unable to fund promised pensions for retired employees. Is that a great business? Just ask the retirees who lost a large part of their pensions or the taxpayers who ultimately paid $49.5 billion to bail the company out from the financial crisis of 2009.

I cannot define what a great company is for you, but I can tell you with absolute certainty that all great companies that stay in business for the long term are nothing more than a collection of systems that consistently maximizes value to all stakeholders in a balanced way.

WANT TO BUILD A GREAT COMPANY? BUILD GREAT SYSTEMS.

At the end of the day, if you're truly committed to creating a great company, you must completely own the idea that at its core your company is nothing more than one giant system composed of a collection of smaller subsystems. Yes, I understand a company has soul, culture, and creativity, but these are all systems in their own right.

The key is to clearly see your company as a collection of four large subsystems that identify and satisfy the needs of the four major stakeholders of your company. Those are:

1. **Customers.** Your customer experience systems
2. **Vendors.** Your vendor-partner systems
3. **Employees.** Your employee systems
4. **Owners.** Your operations and profitability systems

If you own or manage a company that already has rock-solid systems that produce high profit, high growth, a phenomenal workplace, and a phenomenal customer experience, then you can stop reading now. If you think that you don't have time to build systems and work on your business, then you can stop reading now. The fact is, if you cannot make the shift mentally to see yourself as a systems engineer, no book or business-building system can change your situation. Seriously, put the book down and call it a day.

If you own or manage a company that seems to be flat or stuck, if you face the same problems year after year and can't seem to overcome them, or if you want to create a company that's phenomenal for you, your customers, your employees and your vendors, then Section 2 of this book will introduce you to a system for creating those systems.

The Build™ framework was created by running real companies and gathering real life experience, not theories. It's the same system that I use for my companies and the same system that I use to help other business owners develop highly profitable and productive companies.

If you want to be a business owner who truly knows what you're doing, then the remainder of this book is focused on how you can systematically engineer a company that maximizes the value to all the stakeholders in your business. That is to say, this book is going to show you how to create a system that consistently provides:

1. A phenomenal customer experience.
2. A phenomenal workplace.
3. A highly profitable and growing company.
4. A company in which vendors act and are treated like partners.

The only question that remains is: Are you willing to see your company as a system, stop being the hero and embrace the role of systems engineer? If so, let's get started building your company in the next section.

CHAPTER SUMMARY AND ACTION CHECKLIST

- Human error is inevitable, but having systems in place means you have automatic checks and balances to avoid disasters.
- A business is just one big system made of many smaller systems.
- There are four stakeholders in every business: customers, employees, vendors, and owners.
- A great company provides consistent value to all of its stakeholders, not just one or two.
- The best way to monitor how well you're pleasing each stakeholder is to have systems in place that validate your team's efforts.
- Go to coalmarch.com/build to download the resources for this chapter

"An ocean traveler has even more vividly the impression that the ocean is made of waves than that it is made of water."

- Arthur Stanley Eddington

Chapter 5

Build™ A System for Building Systems

If you believe that most service companies are in fact owned and operated by technicians, not leaders, and that these technicians operate companies with no to little integrity, and that these technicians act more like heroes in their businesses instead of system engineers, and that a service company is nothing more than a collection of systems, then one key question remains.

How can you build a service company that consistently:

1. Provides a phenomenal customer experience
2. Is a phenomenal place to work
3. Is a phenomenal cash machine with little to no effort from the owner
4. Is a phenomenal company that the best vendors line up to do business with

What's really being asked is:

How do you transition from a technician-led company to a professionally-led company?

While this may sound trite and a little simplistic, the answer is as simple as the question.

The answer is *systems.*

The only way you'll ever make this transition from a technician-led, low-integrity company to a professionally-led, high-integrity company is through the development of and adherence to high-performing systems.

If, in the past four chapters, you got a glimpse of your own company or of yourself, then the time has come for you to see your company and your role very differently. It's time to see your company as one giant system and to see yourself as the systems engineer.

High-integrity, professional companies believe in systems and they truly understand that systems are the key to their success. They view their role as system engineers and they understand that they need to build systems first, and then hire people to operate the systems, through a well-orchestrated hiring system. That's the key to their success.

If you think or believe that somehow you can skirt this principle and be a great company without systems, procedures, and checklists, then you might as well sign up for the next Sasquatch expedition. The odds of seeing Sasquatch are about the same as your odds of making the transition without systems.

THE BUILD™ SYSTEM IS A PROVEN SYSTEM

The Build™ system is nothing more than a 10-step system designed to help you build your systems. That's right, it's a system for building your systems. Build™ is fast, efficient, time-tested, and proven in multiple service sectors and in multiple markets. It's the same system that I've used to take three service companies from startup to multi-million dollars and it's the same system that I use to help other business owners do the same.

The next 10 steps have been developed through many years of trial and error, experiments that went right and experiments that went wrong, all while doing what I truly love: building companies. Over time we adopted what worked and trashed what didn't.

I don't take all the credit for the success of my companies, but I do take credit for building the systems that attracted capable people and empowered them to build phenomenal companies.

Just like any good system, Build™ is still living and breathing. From time to time we've modified the system as our level of experience and understanding increased. Of course, the changes we make now are very minor compared to when we first started developing the system. I believe this is because we have the right principles and we only update the steps as technology and greater understanding develops.

Build™ is not some college professor's theory, or someone else's thesis. It's not an idea that someone just baked up because it sounded great. Build™ has been developed on the backs of real businesses that deal with the reality of customers, employees, and making payroll every day. This system was developed by real business owners and is in use today by real business owners (myself included.)

ORDER IS IMPORTANT

Years ago, when I attended college, registration was not as simple and easy as it is today. We never had grading stats or reviews on professors. If a class was full, you'd have to physically go to the class on the first day for the very slim possibility that the professor would be kind enough to add you to the class. Most professors wouldn't add you if registration was already full.

The first semester of my freshman year in college, I was late to the registration party and I paid dearly for it. Most of the classes I needed were full and the ones that were open had weird class times. Undeterred, I decided to go to the classes to see if I could get the professors to manually add me.

For each class I visited that day, I was promptly turned away at the door by the professor. Typically there was already a sign on the door that stated, "no manual adds."

As I approached the calculus class that I wanted to take, I knew I had no chance of adding it. Every seat was full and there were even people sitting on the floor. The professor, Dr. Brown, seemed completely at ease with the crowd and began teaching. I almost left because I knew there was no way I was getting into the class, but I decided to stay and take notes anyway.

At the end of class, Dr. Brown made her seemingly irrational registration philosophy quite clear to everyone. With a very thick southern accent, she announced "for y'all who want to add, come see me before you leave so that I can add you. The fact is that, historically, 45% of this class will be gone in the first three weeks. If you struggled in algebra or if you're weak in algebra, you best drop my class now because you'll fail your first exam. This is a calculus course, not an algebra course, and if you ain't good in algebra, then you sure ain't gonna do calculus."

Turns out, Dr. Brown was dead on. After the first exam there were plenty of seats open and her class size dropped to about the same size as any normal course taught at the university.

The story is meant to illustrate a vital point – that as you use Build™ to make your transition from a technician-led company to a professional service company it's extremely important to follow the steps in order.

I, along with other college students, have learned (sometimes the hard way) that you cannot do calculus if you don't have a firm grasp of algebra. The same applies to business. It makes no sense to work on your culture if you haven't taken the time to clearly define what you want that culture to look like. And it makes no sense to build tracking systems if you haven't taken the time to clearly identify which numbers really matter in your business.

Each step in the Build™ framework is built on previous steps and designed to get quick results in the most efficient and effective manner. Don't try to start in the middle or to skip steps. Doing so will at best lead to wasted time and suboptimal results and at worst total system failure.

PROGRESS, PROGRESSIVELY

As a business owner, I tend to want things now, and I typically want to see results immediately. While I know that you probably don't struggle with this, I do. If you have the patience of Job then go ahead and skip to the next section. If you tend to be more like me, then there's something very important that I need to make sure you understand before you start implementing this system.

Have you ever met the perfect person? Have you ever done business with a perfect company? Have you ever had the perfect anything? The answers to these questions are obvious and most business owners have a firm understanding that nothing is ever perfect and nothing ever will be.

Thriving in the midst of chaos is a trait that most successful business owners possess. They understand what's important and what's not. They know how to prioritize and they can be comfortable knowing that while everything is not perfect, the right things are. While others insist on and obsess over perfection, these business owners know how to get results.

I bring this up because this tendency is both a blessing and a curse. As you go through this process, your implementation of each step will never be perfect. Hell, I'm not so sure that I can do each step perfectly and I'm the one writing this book!

However, be sure that you've implemented each step to the point that it's a functioning, living system producing results before you move on to the next step. Don't rush the implementation of Build™. Set benchmarks that must be reached for each system and validate that those benchmarks are met before moving on. Have a philosophy of getting it right the first time and only then moving on.

THERE ARE WORKSHEETS TO HELP YOU ALONG THE WAY

If the idea of building systems seems overwhelming to you or if you are not sure where to start, I have some great news for you. For each step in the Build™ platform there are downloadable PDFs that you can use to build your systems.

These PDFs include simple, step-by-step instructions for how to create and implement Build™. Each PDF also gives you a minimum standard of performance that your system should be producing before you move on to the next step.

You can download the PDFs by going to: www.coalmarch.com/build-resources

There's also an active community of business owners just like you who're in the process of transitioning their companies from a technician company to a professional company. You can connect with them at: www.coalmarch.com/build

THE BUILD™ SYSTEM IS A MEANS TO AN END

Have you ever had an argument with someone, only to find that, once you calmed down, you couldn't remember exactly why you started arguing in the first place? We're all guilty of this in some form or fashion. Too often we get so caught up in expressing our viewpoint or proving that we're right that we completely forget the very thing that we disagreed about in the first place. Our focus somehow changes from what we were originally trying to accomplish to simply winning an argument.

Of course, I am not a psychologist or therapist and I'm not here to solve any relationship or emotional problems. I only bring this up because there are times that we as humans tend to confuse the means with the ends.

The Build™ system is nothing more than a basic system to create your systems. That's it, nothing more. Build™ is the means. The end is a company that produces phenomenal results for all four stakeholders: owner(s), customers, vendors and employees.

This may seem like a simple and straightforward concept, but after going through this process with several companies, I can tell you that sometimes the end gets lost in the means.

I've seen companies really take on this idea of systemization to the degree that they create an imbalance. You know these companies. They're the companies that tend to quote policy to you instead of taking care of you as a customer. Essentially, these companies allowed systems – the means – to get in the way of the end – a phenomenal customer experience. On the other side, I've seen companies create systems only to put them on a shelf and never look at them again.

The key is to always keep the end in mind as you go through the Build™ process. Don't become a system zealot and don't create systems that no one follows. Create systems that produce results for all four stakeholders, no one else. At times you may need to deviate from a system, while at other times you will need to adhere to your system with an iron fist.

Ultimately your company must meet the relevant needs, through systems, of everyone involved. If you're not meeting all your stakeholders' needs then your systems are not working and you need to change them.

CHAPTER SUMMARY AND ACTION CHECKLIST

- Systems make the difference between a technician-led company and a professionally-led company.
- Good things come to those who wait. Treat each step like its own system — implement one at a time, in order, and wait for each one to function well before adding the next.
- Don't let your systems become the end-all, be-all of your business. You are in charge. You decide when changes need to happen, how they need to happen, or when policies or procedures need to take a back seat in a unique situation.
- Go to coalmarch.com/build to download the resources for this chapter

"I'm just preparing my impromptu remarks."

- Winston Churchill

Chapter 6

Step 1:

Set the Vision

Imagine for a moment that one afternoon you're lounging on your couch in your underwear, binge watching the latest season of Game of Thrones when unexpectedly you hear a knock at your door.

You quickly throw on some old shorts and a T-shirt and open your door to what seems to be a party. All of a sudden someone screams, "Surprise! You've won the $250 million Publisher's Clearing House Sweepstakes!" Everyone is screaming, laughing, crying. You even get your picture taken next to one of those ridiculously large checks with the words "250 Million Dollars" emblazoned across the front.

A few months later, after your celebrity status has worn off and you've isolated yourself from all of your "new friends" who just happen to need a little money seeing as now you're a millionaire, you decide that it's time to get down to business and build a wonderful home for you and your family.

You hire a home building consultant who helps you hire the very best contractors in town. You hire the very best framers, the very best electricians, the very best plumbers, the very best interior designers, and the list goes on and on until at last you have a full staff of professionals ready to build your new wonderful home.

On the day that construction is set to begin, you have a large meeting with all of the "very best" professionals and you explain that you want a wonderful home for you and your family and their job is to do their very best to build it. Undoubtedly the team of the "very best" professionals that you've assembled can deliver whatever your imagination can think of, regardless of how absurd or outlandish your ideas may be. After your moving speech about wanting a wonderful home, you finish off with a rally cry of, "let's do this, we've got three months!"

The room fills with silence. Even the crickets aren't chirping. This is not the response you were expecting. What are these people doing? Why aren't they working? Where's their enthusiasm? Where's their drive? These people are professionals and you're paying a premium for their services. Instead of building your wonderful home, they're all just sitting there staring at you with blank faces.

Finally, the landscape contractor asks the question, "do you want a pool?" Of course, you answer. All wonderful homes have a pool. Then the plumber jumps in, "wait, you want a pool? Pools are a pain, they leak and they require too much maintenance. People rarely use them and when they do, they just pee in them." Then the electrician jumps in. "Pools are great. You can put some really cool LED lights in them and they're wonderful for hosting late night parties, especially with the right lighting." That's when the framer just loses it. "No pool is complete without a fully furnished pool house complete with a man-cave – that should be the priority here. This guy is a millionaire, he needs a man cave at the pool!"

As the fight ensues between the contractors, you have the sinking realization that none of them have any idea what a wonderful home means to you nor what it should look like. They all have different ideas, they all believe that their ideas are right and they're intent on convincing everyone else why their idea is the right one. No way are they going to get done in three months. No way at all.

THE FALLACY OF THE ASSUMED

It seems unthinkable that anyone, no matter how much money they had, would ever begin a project such as building a home without a complete set of blueprints.

This story, while somewhat unrealistic, illustrates a critical point: Most small service companies, even some large ones, operate just like our group of contractors who are building that "wonderful home" with no plans whatsoever.

Owners and their managers at the typical small service company hire the top professionals, train them on the technical work of the business and then assume that these professionals know exactly what the owners and managers are trying to build. These companies have no vision, and the few that do seldom communicate it. They just assume that these professionals should know what they're building.

These service companies are no different than the contractors in our story. Everyone at the company has their own idea of how the company should look, what it should be focused on, and what should be important. With the lack of clarity, owners, managers, and even the frontline employees begin to spend more time arguing about what the outcomes should look like and why their ideas are right rather than doing productive work.

These owners and managers assume that it is self-evident that everyone should sell, everyone should be nice to customers, everyone should look presentable, and so on. The end result is a company without clarity, where it takes longer to do things, it's more expensive, and the service is different depending on who does the work.

The fact is that, as a service company, you hire people. And people, unlike widgets, have their own ideas of how things should be, how you should be, how the company should be, and how other employees should be. Without a guiding vision of what your "wonderful business" should look like, you and your managers will do nothing more than the equivalent of herding arguing cats around every day. It's as exhausting as it is unnecessary.

Creating a vision for yourself and for your company is the first step in the Build™ platform because it must be. It's impossible to know where you're going if you haven't gotten clear on the destination and the rules of the trip. It's impossible to ever know if you've arrived or if you're making progress if you aren't clear on the destination.

It's not my job or the prerogative of this book to tell you who your company should be and where your company should go. I'm only making the point that without a vision, it's impossible to build a phenomenal company that can satisfy the needs of all four stakeholders: customers, employees, vendors and owners.

THE REALITIES OF CRAFTING A VISION

Once upon a time, a young man seeking to know all things moved to a cave in the mountains to study with a guru. He wanted, he said, to learn everything there was to know about life and about the world. The guru supplied him with stacks of books and left him alone so he could study.

Every morning, the guru returned to the cave to monitor the young man's progress. In his hand, he carried a heavy wooden walking stick. Each morning, he asked him the same question: "have you learned everything there is to know about life and about the world yet?"

Each morning, his answer was the same. "No," he said, "I haven't." The guru would then deliver a hard blow to the head of the young man with his walking stick. This scenario repeated itself for months.

One day the guru entered the cave, asked the same question, heard the same answer, and raised his walking stick to strike the young man in the same way, but the young man grabbed the walking stick from the guru, stopping his assault in midair.

Relieved to end the daily batterings but fearing reprisal, the young man looked up at the guru. To his surprise, the guru smiled. "Congratulations," he said, "you have graduated. You now know everything you need to know about life and about the world."

"How's that?" the young man asked.

"You have learned that you will never learn everything there is to know," he replied. "And you have learned how to stop the pain."

This chapter is about just that. Stopping the pain. Most companies operate without any vision and it's killing them. Each day is rife with customer issues, employee issues, and financial issues, among many more. These are all symptoms of a much larger problem: no vision.

If you want to know all there is to know about starting, building, and operating a phenomenal company, the answers are as unique as the grains of sand on a beach. There are multiple ways to do this and no specific way is the one right way. The key is knowing what you need to know.

What do you need to know? I can't answer that for you.

What I can tell you is that all phenomenal companies have a vision and their people don't just know it. They live it everyday.

I believe a lot of business owners often neglect and even reject the idea of creating a vision for their companies because they feel, just like the young man in the story, that they need to know all there is to know about what's going to happen in the future. It's impossible to know that. All you need to know is what the ideal looks like and then take action towards making that ideal become reality.

Just like what the guru taught the young man in the cave, it's all about what you need to know right now versus knowing all things. This is to say:

Creating your vision is about the process of thinking, it's not about knowing all things.

YOUR PERSONAL VISION

Have you ever met someone who seemed to be a workaholic? I'm not talking about a hard working person but a person who, for whatever reason, dedicates and defines their entire life around their work or company? These are the people who seem to live at – and only live for – work.

How many friends do they have? How many vacations do they take? How creative are they? How happy do these people seem to be?

The answers to these questions are obvious. Most workaholics didn't start that way. Most start at a company with the idea of contributing their very best but then over the months and years seem to confuse their "best" with their "time." It's as if they've lost themselves in their work. Why is that?

This may seem like an odd place to start, especially considering that this is a book about how to build your business, but before you begin the process of building a phenomenal company, first you need to get clear on what's most important in your life and how your business will support that.

Phenomenal service companies are built and created by phenomenal people. Phenomenal people know who they are, where they're going, how they will get there, and what it will look like once they have arrived. It's impossible to build a phenomenal company with visionless, purposeless people.

Phenomenal people understand that the business is there to support their life; they understand that their lives are not the business. The business is a component, but not their entire life. Giving the business that kind of power is irresponsible and moves a phenomenal person to a mediocre one at best, a bitter and resentful one at worst.

Creating a vision for yourself will help you clarify exactly what's important to you, what your ideal life looks like, and how the business will support that. This clarity is the very thing that may save your life.

Personally, I think workaholics and poor performers are people who either don't have a personal vision or who have lost touch with it. Visionless people make the worst employers and the worst employees. Their priorities are constantly shifting. They believe that they exist for the business and they're willing to give everything they have to the business (which the business glady accepts, if you allow it).

A personal vision is nothing more than a road map of what your life would look like if everything were ideal. It's a written document of who you are, what you're about, what's important to you, and what that all looks like.

Of course, nothing in our life is ever ideal and it never will be. The trick is to move closer to your ideal without being discouraged if you miss it. Even if you do miss, you'll be in a better place than if you'd never moved in that direction at all. If you don't have clarity as to what the ideal looks like, you'll never make progress towards it. Your personal vision is a road map that protects you from getting completely and totally engulfed in the day-to-day while providing you with the clarity to make progress towards your ideal.

The first step of Build™ is all about you, and it's completely OK to be selfish. You must demand that the business support your life. I'm not just talking about from a financial perspective, but from a professional, social, self-development perspective as well. The business is a means to help you improve in most areas of your life. If it doesn't, then you're doing it wrong. Of course there will be times when you'll have to give more of yourself to business and other times when you must give more of yourself to some other area of your life, but never lose sight of this simple fact:

The business exists to support you, not the other way around.

THE COMPANY VISION

The purpose of every business is to make money. Period. If you want to save the world, join a non-profit. If you want to further a cause, join a social organization. If you enjoy some technical work then go to work for someone else. If you want to own or manage a business, your purpose is to make money first. Never lose sight of this basic truth.

Oftentimes business owners and managers confuse their purpose with their vision. Your purpose is what you're doing. Your *vision* is how you're doing it. There's a very big difference between the two.

Creating a written company vision is a way to unify everyone at your company on the "how" you do business. It's a way to make sure that your own proverbial plumbers, electricians, and framers are clear on what they're building (the vision), and what it should look like. It's a way to ensure that everyone in your boat is paddling in the same direction.

Your company vision is nothing more than a document that clearly defines:

1. Who you are as a company
2. What values your company stands for
3. Where your company is going
4. How your company will get there

The idea is to create a document, a credo, that people can understand, get behind, and be a part of. It's a way to get people to stop spending time on trying to figure out what the ideal is, and instead start working on making the ideal a reality.

Getting clear on who you are and what you're doing through a vision is one of the greatest gifts that you can give to yourself and to your team because it allows everyone to work together and it puts everyone on the same track.

YOUR VISION - REVISITED

Just for a moment, I want you to think about how many messages you've read and ignored since you woke up this morning. How many messages do you get and ignore in an entire day? If you had to guess how many messages you must filter in one day, what would your guess be?

Chances are, if you're a business owner or a manager, the answer to this question is, "a lot." There's that marketing email about how you can get a special 10% off discount for a limited time only. Then there's the person who feels that it's their personal mission to include you in every email chain that has nothing directly to do with you. And let's not forget that request from the Nigerian prince who just needs a little cash to unlock millions of dollars that he's willing to share with you for a simple investment of a hundred dollars or so. Just wire him some funds today so that he can gain access to his millions and make you a millionaire along the way.

My point here is that, in today's world, trying to read and comprehend all of the messages directed at us is like trying to drink water from a firehose. It's impossible. Just to get anything done in today's information overload reality we must learn how to filter and identify what's important from what's not important, then move on and take action.

This ability to filter information quickly, while very useful, also has a downside. Many of us, myself included, remember nothing (we have our hard drives and Google for that), don't fully read things (because we're in a hurry to get through all of the other messages), and don't think critically about what we just read or heard because the majority of our brain is working on filtering all this information, not focusing on the content.

The fact is that in today's world there is noise, and a lot of it.

Taking the time to think about, craft, and put to paper a vision for yourself and for your company is one of the most important and critical steps that you can ever take as a person and business owner.

But you're not done. Your vision and the time that you took to create it is a complete waste if you don't create a system to consistently review it and question it. Don't make a vision, put it on a plaque, place it on the wall, and think the exercise is over.

I've now owned one of my service companies for over 12 years and our vision has changed every year. Of course, in the latter years the changes were minor, but there were changes nonetheless.

Having a vision is great but it is totally meaningless if you don't think about it and do your best to live it. To think about and live your vision you must find a way to make sure that it doesn't end up as another momentary note in the endless noise of your life or the lives of those associated with your company.

There's an old marketing axiom that states that a person must hear something 7 times before they remember it. From my own experience, especially regarding my vision, I think that number is grossly inadequate.

In today's day and age, if you want your staff – and yourself as well – to know and remember your vision, you're going to have to talk about it and refer back to it almost weekly. At my companies, any training we do, any program we do, any change we make, we find a way to tie it back to our vision and we talk about it.

While I can't tell you a magic number of times you should be communicating and training on your vision, both to yourself and to your employees, I personally use the eye roll method. Meaning that when I start talking about the vision and I see people rolling their eyes and asking "do we have to talk about this again," then I know that people understand and remember the vision. This tells me our vision is making it past the noise.

Another reason to read your vision often is that you want to be sure that it's a living, breathing document. The priorities you have as a 20-year-old are very different from the priorities you have as a 40-year-old. And the priorities you have a 40-year-old are very different than the priorities you have as a 60-year-old.

The point is that while your vision, for the most part, should contain steadfast principles and ideals, your priorities and focus will change as you and your company changes. And your vision has to shift with those changes.

GETTING STARTED

As I mentioned earlier, the Build™ framework is a system for creating your systems. As such, you don't have to reinvent the wheel and you don't have to do this alone.

If you don't know how to get started in creating your own personal vision, or a vision for your company, we have downloadable PDFs that you can use to get started.

To download these PDFs, just go to coalmarch.com/build and look for chapter 6 resources. There are worksheets to help you through the process of creating your own personal vision as well as the vision for your company or department.

CHAPTER SUMMARY AND ACTION CHECKLIST

- Everyone has an opinion, but yours is the only one that matters. Know what you want out of your business, and your life, and make it clear to the people around you. Don't let their judgement cloud yours.
- Your business exists to support you, not the other way around.
- Just like a person without vision, a company without vision isn't going to go far. Take the time to figure out what your company stands for, where you want it to go, and how you want it to get there, then write it all down.
- You can change your vision over time, as long as you change your systems to reflect it.
- Go to coalmarch.com/build to download the resources for this chapter

"Everything in our strategy our competitors could copy tomorrow..... but they can't copy the culture - and they know it."

- Herb Kelleher,

Founder, Southwest Airlines

Chapter 7

Step 2:

Create a Culture of Performance

While this may seem like a step back, it's worth our time to revisit one basic, fundamental truth because it sets the stage for the entire chapter. That principle is:

> **The only real measurements of success in your business are profits and cash, nothing else.**

I understand that there is more to business than profit. I understand that there is more to business than cash. I understand supporting your family is important. I understand that the people who work for you are important. I understand that our environment is important. I understand all of these things and yet the principle remains that if your business cannot generate sufficient profit or doesn't have the cash to pay the bills, your ability to affect any of the above issues is effectively nullified.

Have you ever seen an iceberg in real life? Icebergs are nothing more than large freshwater ice packs that have broken off of a glacier or ice shelf. Icebergs are some of nature's most beautiful formations of water, wind, and ice. While these formations are beautiful, they only represent about 9% of the entire iceberg. That's because 91% of the iceberg is completely submerged under water.

To the average observer, a distant iceberg may seem a small, insignificant, beautiful piece of floating ice. To the seasoned maritime sailor, any iceberg that can be seen above water is considered a major hazard because he or she knows the majority of the iceberg can't be seen.

I want you, for a moment, to visualize your business as an iceberg. That is to say, just like the tip of an iceberg, profit is only the visible result of your company. Everything that your company does, everything it doesn't do, everything that it is, and everything that it is not, is measured by profit, the tip. Likewise, just like an iceberg, the vast majority of a business is not represented by this visible cap. There are employees, customers, inventory, insurance, etc. Concretely stated, it's the 91% that makes the 9% possible.

In this chapter, we're going to go underwater to explore the iceberg.

That is to say, we're going to explore probably the largest lever you can possibly pull to drive profit in your company: your culture.

If you can get the culture right, your company will be highly profitable and a breeze to manage. Get it wrong and you'll be scraping by and hate coming to work every day. For every service company, whether it's medical services, lawn care, pest control, plumbing or anything in between, your culture is by far the most critical component that drives your profitability as a company and your job satisfaction as an owner or manager.

Visually, this is what your company looks like.

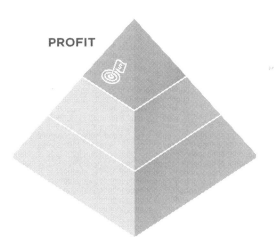

PROFIT

HOW PROFIT IS MADE IN A SERVICE COMPANY

Have you ever met a service company owner or manager that obsesses over minor expenses in the business? You know who these people are. These are the guys that turn the thermostat to

85 in the summer and 65 in the winter. These are the guys who will not pay for company snacks. These are the guys who will send a long-trusted vendor packing for a $0.30 price difference. These are the guys who refuse to pay much above minimum wage for employees because in their minds, they must keep expenses low.

Years ago, I was asked by a friend and service business owner, who in many regards was just like the owner I described above, to take a fresh look at his business. He was getting older and was looking to sell his business in the next 3-5 years. He'd been trying to solve the same problem for over 5 years but just couldn't seem to overcome it.

His company had always been highly profitable as compared to industry averages but since his company had grown substantially, his profit fell and stabilized at the 12% mark. No matter what he did, year after year, he couldn't get above that mark, even though companies roughly the same size in the same industry were consistently earning more than 20% profit. This inability to boost his profit concerned him, especially since he knew that having a lower than expected profit margin would ultimately result in a lower price for his company when he eventually sold.

When I started digging into his company, almost everything looked healthy and normal. His leads and his sales were growing year after year and he was doing a wonderful job in keeping his administration expenses very low. His company was a success. It was growing and it was profitable, but the fact that my friend couldn't get his profit to industry standards bothered him.

My friend, a frugal but good guy nonetheless, practiced what I call the "low ball" method to managing payroll. That is to say, on average he paid his employees 60%-70% of what they could be making working for a competitor. He adopted this practice 25 years earlier when he couldn't afford to pay market price for employees. Now, years later, his business was much larger and much more sophisticated. But he was following the same salary principle he adopted when he started the business.

While hiring and managing low-salaried employees seemed to work in the early years, it was totally and completely backfiring on him now. His business had grown to more than $3 Million in revenue and it was all but impossible for him to be involved in daily operations. Knowing this, he hired managers to help him manage the chaos. As with his front line employees, my friend also low-balled his managers as well, hiring them at 60-70% of market value.

After going through my friend's profit and loss statement, the only number that seemed out of place was his payroll. His payroll expense was more than 12% higher than the industry average. When I highlighted this to him he was completely unconvinced that he had a problem.

My friend kept asking me, "How in the hell do I have a payroll issue? You see what the people around here make, don't you, Donnie? I'm not wasting money in payroll!" In his mind, it was totally impossible to have a payroll problem when his practice was to lowball employees, but just as John Adams once famously said, "Facts are stubborn things".

Although my friend paid bottom feeder pay to his employees, he had a lot of them. To the tune of 50% more employees than other companies of equal size. He told me that for the past five years, as the company continued growing, his managers had to hire more technicians to get all of the work done.

Luckily, my friend wanted to take action. So when I recommended that we go into the field to see what his people were actually doing, he was happy to comply. Once we started observing his technicians, the answer to his payroll problem became abundantly clear. Throughout the day, as we randomly dropped in on technicians, we observed the following:

1. A technician sleeping in his service truck.
2. Most technicians only scheduled for 5 hours of work in an 8 hour work day.
3. Technicians completing stops without bothering to actually do the work.
4. Technicians who spent almost an hour on the phone with the home office gossiping about how – get this – another employee wasn't pulling his weight. (I'm sure that it never crossed their minds that they were as equally unproductive.)

5. Technicians showing up late to appointments.
6. Managers taking 2 hour lunches.

In the final analysis, my friend didn't have a payroll problem, he had a productivity problem.

All the many years of low employee pay and high employee turnover had completely decimated the culture of his business. Most of his employees were the bottom of the barrel type who were not looking to start a career at his company more than they were looking for someone to hire them – they wanted a job, not a career. The employees who lasted longer than a year became very good at justifying to themselves that their low productivity was due to their low pay.

His business and his culture had become a magnet for low-producing employees who hired more low-producing employees to get all of the work done, because they sure were not going to do it. Simply stated, he had a full–blown downward spiral of dumb people hiring more dumb people to not work.

While my friend was "saving" money by paying his employees below market price, in reality it was costing him dearly. When you think about it, what type of potential employees are attracted to a company that pays 60-70% of market value? What do you think these employees will do if they feel like they're being compensated unfairly? What do you think the good employees will do when they're offered positions at companies with a higher salary?

As a service company, it's true that your largest expense on your profit and loss statement is your payroll, but payroll management is not the source of profitability – productivity is.

As a service company, the only thing you sell is time. The technicians' time, office staff's time, and your time, all make up the largest expense on your payroll. This is a critical point. You cannot simply set a payroll budget percentage and follow it. Just like you cannot ignore what your payroll percentage is.

If you want a phenomenal company and phenomenal profitability, then you must view your service company through the lense of productivity, not payroll percentages, like my friend did. Visually this looks like:

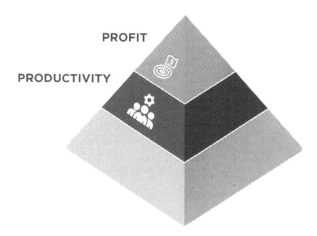

Don't misunderstand what I am saying here. I'm in no way suggesting that you offer your customers substandard service, nor am I advocating overloading your employees to the point of breaking them. What I am suggesting is that you view your profitability as a function of how you empower your employees to provide the best service possible in the least amount of time.

So if profit is a function of productivity, just how can you maximize productivity?

PRODUCTIVITY IS A RESULT OF CULTURE, NOT STRATEGY

Have you ever returned from a business conference with a great idea only to have it become DOA (dead on arrival)? I'm not talking about a small idea, I'm talking about a really transformative idea that would completely change your company. Have you ever tried to implement an idea like this only to see that weeks later no one even remembers what the idea was?

Why is that? How is it that even though you have a new and better strategy, for some reason, it just doesn't seem to take off?

I ask these questions because many business owners and managers truly believe that if they had the right business strategy their businesses would grow, their employees would love them, their customers would love them, and their companies would be wildly profitable. It's as if the right strategy would result in a "We Are the World" concert right in their own company.

The belief that the right strategy is what makes a company successful, highly profitable, and highly productive is dead wrong.

Strategy is a set of techniques that you use to compete with other businesses and acquire customers. Strategy can and must change as market conditions and customer preferences change. Strategies are fluid, and in some cases, especially in the tech industry, must be revisited on a monthly basis.

Culture, on the other hand, is very different from strategy. Culture is more concerned with how your people work, how your people interact with customers, and how your employees view their role in your organization. Culture is built over a period of years and decades.

Oftentimes, we as business owners and managers get into trouble when we focus on strategy after strategy to increase profitability without any thought or attention given to the culture of our companies.

While having a winning strategy is extremely important to creating a sustainable and profitable company, having a flawless strategy is not enough.

Imagine for a moment that you just returned from a vacation of a lifetime. Your travels took you to the most exotic places in the world and you took thousands upon thousands of pictures and video to remember this truly once-in-a-lifetime special experience.

As you return home, reality sets in that you now have the laborious task of organizing and categorizing your photos so that you can highlight the best experiences from this once in a lifetime vacation.

You decide that if you're going to get this done in your lifetime, you're going to have to get a software program designed to make it easy for you to find the photos that allow you to tell the story of your vacation and pick out the important highlights. After an exhaustive search online and hours of scouring product reviews, you decide on the most expensive software because you believe it will do the best job and save you time.

After purchasing the expensive software, you download it and run the installer for the program. Everything's going fine with installation until all of a sudden your computer completely crashes. After several attempts to install the new program, you discover, much to your dismay, that while the program you just tried to install seemed amazing, your underlying operating system has a major flaw and can't run the program.

Strategy and culture are no different than this software example. Undoubtedly to succeed in business you must have a sound strategy, but before any strategy can work, your underlying operating system, your culture, must be solid and capable of actually executing the strategy. Without a great culture, even the best and most successful strategies cannot and will not work.

Jack Welch, arguably one of the most successful CEOs ever to run a company in the United States, spent an unprecedented 30 years at the helm of G.E. In an age where CEOs are hired and then subsequently fired like pop-culture movie stars, Jack Welch managed to not only keep his job as CEO of one of the largest corporations in the world for over 30 years, but also increased the value of the company over 4000%. Mind you, these are not start up numbers.

The burning question to ask is, how did he do it?

In a recent interview, Jack Welch answered this very question. When asked about his amazing performance at G.E., Jack stated, "I spent 80% of my time on culture, not strategy." Likewise, he also stated that his biggest mistakes usually involved making acquisitions based on numbers and not on culture.

What Jack understood, and what many business owners and managers routinely miss, is this: High profit is a function of high productivity. High productivity is a function of culture first, then strategy. Returning to our triangle:

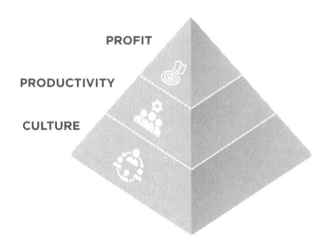

LIKE IT OR NOT, YOU ALREADY HAVE A CULTURE

So what is culture? In the context of our discussion, culture is nothing more than a set of beliefs and behaviors that determine how your company interacts with customers, employees, vendors, and owners.

Whether or not you realize it, whether or not you understand it, whether or not you pay attention to it, your company already has a culture. It doesn't matter if your company has two employees or two hundred, if you have an employee, you have a culture.

Put more simply, culture is what all stakeholders believe and how they act when they're in your company.

Oftentimes culture is not expressly defined but develops over time from the cumulative traits of the people the company hires.

If you have not already figured this out by this point, I'm going to get very explicit in stating it now. If you get nothing else from this chapter, get this:

Your company's culture is the most important aspect of operating a profitable company because it leads to high productivity, which in turn leads to high profit.

CREATING THE RIGHT CULTURE – EASY QUESTIONS, HARD ANSWERS

So if profit, like an iceberg, is the result of the underlying productivity, and productivity is a function of culture, then there are a few questions that you'll need to answer:

1. How do I create a culture centered on productivity?
2. What's the best culture for a service company?
3. How do I build a culture?
4. Can I change my culture?
5. How can I be intentional about building the right culture?

I have both good news and even better news. The good news is that there are proven and predictable answers to every one of these questions. The even better news is that the answers are in the chapters that follow and are at the core of the Build™ Platform.

The purpose of Build™ is to help you create a company that provides a phenomenal place to work, a phenomenal customer experience, a phenomenal company that vendors want to do business with and a company that produces phenomenal profit.

I promise you that if you seriously commit yourself and your company to implementing Build™, by its very nature, your culture will transition to become a highly productive culture. But before we move on to the next chapter, I want to be sure that I address one more fundamental issue.

If you're serious about building a culture of disciplined productivity don't underestimate the power of you. It all begins with you.

Can you imagine a company of disciplined, highly productive front-line employees built with undisciplined and unfocused managers? Likewise, can you imagine a company with highly focused and highly productive managers built with undisciplined and unfocused leaders and owners? The answer to these questions is obvious.

I bring this up because every now and then I meet an owner or manager who believes that somehow they can create a disciplined company but shortcut the process. They say, "yes, I want a highly profitable and highly productive company but I will delegate getting there to someone else." If you think that culture building can be delegated to someone else I want you to consider how for 30 years Jack Welch didn't delegate building a culture and he led a multi-billion dollar corporation. He knew that it all started with himself.

In the previous chapter, we reviewed creating a vision for yourself and for your company. Vision is the first step so that you can get clear on who you are, who your company is, what kind of culture you want and how you plan to build it. It's impossible to create a disciplined culture if you don't know what it looks like as a leader. If you haven't completed your vision yet, do it now, as everything, including building a culture, depends on the clarity of your vision.

In the end, companies that have a great, well-defined culture but poor strategies will always do better than companies with perfect strategies but a poor culture.

The good news is that culture building is probably the most productive and potent work you'll do as a leader. If you have the right operating system, you can run the best programs in the world and they'll work, while those without a proper operating system will fail. Culture first, then strategy. It's that simple and you'll have both the freedom and flexibility to change strategies, fix mistakes, and outdo the competition every time. Culture is simply that important.

CHAPTER SUMMARY AND ACTION CHECKLIST

- Just as a glacier is more than just the peak above water, a business is more than just the service it provides. A phenomenal business is made up of phenomenal people, and it's your job to attract them and build them up.
- People are your greatest expense precisely because they are your greatest asset. Invest in them now and it will pay dividends over the long term.
- Happy employees produce more and better work, and their happiness is a direct result of the culture you foster at your company.
- Culture doesn't just happen. You have to build it just like you'd build any other system.
- Go to coalmarch.com/build to download the resources for this chapter.

"**Rank does not confer privilege or give power. It imposes responsibility.**"

— **Peter Drucker**

Chapter 8

Step 3:

Define Who is Doing What

Have you ever watched a soccer game with five and six year old players? It's like watching someone trying to herd cats around a field. There are moments of drama (usually from the parents), moments of triumph, moments of rage, and moments of complete and utter humiliation. These small but enthusiastic players have little understanding and experience of the game of soccer but their enthusiasm and emotion makes for some of the best parental entertainment that you'll ever experience.

With four children of my own, I've probably sat through more than fifty little league soccer games (and I'm still not done; with games, that is). One thing that I've observed in watching these games is that if you've seen one little league soccer game, you've seen them all.

Once the referee blows the whistle to start the game, two factions emerge from the players on both teams. Faction one are the players who really have no interest in soccer. These are the kids that are staring off into space, kicking an ant hill or playing tag with players on the opposing team.

Faction two players are the kids that have a ton of enthusiasm but no structure on how to play the game. You know who these kids are because they're the ones that chase the ball all over the field. To these kids the only objective is to chase the ball and kick it. Results don't really matter; as long as there's action, they are "in the game".

All four of my kids played soccer growing up and I've seen both good and bad teams along the way. One of my daughters played for two years on a team that never won a single game. In her third year of playing, my daughter was randomly placed on another team with a coach named Pug (I am not making that up, that really was his name).

On the first day of practice, I could tell that this season was going to be different and that I was going to like Pug a lot. He explained to the kids on the team that they were not there to win any games. In fact, he couldn't care less whether they won or lost every game for the entire season (how's that for building up the self-esteem of the kids on your team). Instead, Pug stated that the primary reason that the kids were there was to learn how to have fun playing soccer, not win games.

At the end of this inspiring speech, Pug then turned to the parents and said "if any of you disagree with my philosophy of learning to have fun versus winning games, I am more than happy to help your daughter get placed on another team". A couple of parents who wanted to protect the self-esteem of their kids took Pug up on his offer. Amused and hopeful, I was ecstatic that my daughter would get to play for Pug.

If you've ever tried to teach a five or six year old anything, you know that attention spans are measured in seconds, not hours or even minutes. In the years of observing my kids play soccer, I can tell you that the coaches were just as predictable as the players.

Each year the coaches would explain what the positions were in the game, have scrimmage games to show the positions in action, and run drills to reinforce what was taught. Of course, at game time all of this "teaching" and "organization" would go out the door and the kids would not play their positions but would instead chase the ball all over the field no matter which area of the field the ball was in. It was not uncommon for the goalie to be on the wrong side of the field.

After his non-motivational speech, Coach Pug did something that I'll never forget. Instead of starting the normal practice drills that all of the other coaches typically do, Pug pulled colored wristbands from his gym bag and then placed the kids into the playing positions on the soccer field. He then explained to the kids, "if you want actual playing time at our games, you must first learn your position and how to play it. If you don't learn this, you can practice until you do, but you cannot play."

Pug then took the colored wristbands and placed them on the wrist of each player in a position on the field. For example, the left wing wore a blue wristband on her left wrist. The right wing wore a blue wristband on her right wrist. Each player had a position and each position had a specific wristband.

Pug had created a visual cue to remind the kids of what position they played and what side of the field they should be on to keep them on track during the practices and games. These tiny little wristbands were enough to remind the kids to not chase the ball but to instead play their position. Each practice Pug reminded the kids to look at their wrists and then get where they needed to be on the field.

The result from Pug's wristband teaching system was a disciplined, organized team of players who understood their responsibilities on the field. Even though Pug had no shining stars on the team that year, his players went undefeated both in the regular season and in the end of season tournament.

At the conclusion of the tournament win, Pug congratulated the kids not for winning the tournament, but for learning how to play soccer, for having fun and for fulfilling their responsibilities to the team. I was both amazed and impressed that one simple change to help the kids understand their roles and responsibilities made all the difference between a losing team and an undefeated team.

So why are we even discussing little league soccer? What does little league soccer have to do with building a service company? The reason is that in my years of building my own service companies and helping others do the same, I have observed the following:

Most service companies operate like a little league soccer team.

That is to say, most employees are assigned a position and given a title, but once the whistle blows they end up chasing the ball like everyone else. The belief is that as long as someone looks busy and seems engaged in some aspect of the business then that person is a valuable resource for the company and producing results. Never-mind whether the person is doing anything that's actually helping the company. They're busy, they're working hard. That's what's important and that's all that matters.

KNOWING WHAT REALLY NEEDS TO BE DONE

In our age, being busy has evolved into a social status symbol. You want to look like a freak in a social setting? Just tell everyone how you're not really that busy and watch what happens. My guess is that you'll get looks of disgust and looks of indignation and probably everything in between. Most people assume that if you're not busy then you're not important because important people are busy.

Because of this assumed fact, that important people are busy, most people truly want to be busy and have the feeling that they are accomplishing things for themselves and their companies. The problem is that the majority of workers, especially in small companies, are caught up in the thick of thin things, chasing the ball like our five and six year old soccer players.

The problem is caused by the fact that most owners and managers of service companies never stop to take the time to clearly define the results that really matter and those that don't. They don't clearly describe who has responsibility for what, and who does not. They don't define clear standards of how they want things done. Ultimately in most service companies there's a lack of clearly defined positions and the results that each position should produce.

What's an employee to do? Can you really blame them? When was the last time you read the job descriptions for the positions at your company? How clear are they?

EFFICIENCY THROUGH CLARITY

Many years ago I had a client who owned a mid-sized service company in Orlando, Florida. Even though his business was growing at 10% year over year, his profit was withering each year and he now faced serious cash flow issues.

After going through his numbers we discovered that his revenue per employee was significantly lower than the average for his industry.

Revenue per employee is a quick and easy way to measure the efficiency and productivity of a business, though in some cases it can be misleading if your pricing is not in line with industry averages.

In my client's case, his pricing was actually higher than the industry average. When I confronted him about his low revenue per employee and his premium pricing, he replied, "Donnie, I already have most of my employees working more than 50 hours a week, how can I possibly ask them to do more?"

I then asked him to walk me through his organizational (org) chart. The conversation went like this:

Me: Can I have a copy of your org chart?
Client: Well, I don't really have an org chart, seems like a waste of time to me. Everyone knows who reports to who here.

Me: OK, how many techs do you have?
Client: 8, why?

Me: Who do they report to?
Client: Well, they hmm…. Well they report to George.

Me: So, George writes their reviews and grades them?
Client: Um, well not really, I write the technician's reviews.

Me: OK, so George hires and fires technicians for you?
Client: Um, well not really. I make the call on who we hire and

who we fire. I do talk to George though before I do anything.

Me: OK, so George trains your technicians for you?
Client: Not really, I run our training meetings. George does ride with our technicians though to make sure that they are doing a good job.

Me: OK, so what does George do exactly?
Client: Well he helps the techs when they have a problem

We repeated this same conversation for every single area of his business. His service department, his sales department, and even his customer service department. When all of the dust settled, it was clear that essentially every single employee reported to him – every single one.

Since he didn't have an organizational chart with clearly defined responsibilities, his managers were not really managers at all – they were nothing more than higher-paid front-line employees. These managers had it made. They had the title, they had the prestige, they had the pay. What they didn't have was responsibility. They were having their cake and eating it too.

The owner, on the other hand, had all of the responsibility. In addition to the responsibility of operating the company, he was buried with hiring, firing, writing people up, training, writing reviews, and even driving key projects in the company.

The result of having more responsibilities than humanly possible to manage was that he sucked at all of them. He was so overloaded and overwhelmed, he couldn't spare a fraction of the necessary time to get good results for each responsibility. The wrong people were being hired, his employees were not getting feedback on how they could improve, and training was non-existent.

This owner didn't really have a profitability problem, he had a responsibility problem. As his business grew, instead of thinking through exactly what needed to be done and who would bear the responsibility of doing it, he just operated his business the way he'd always done from the days when he only had five employees.

Over time, not getting clear on what needed to be done and who would do it essentially transformed his business from robust and healthy to a broken company that couldn't pay its bills, was miserable to operate, miserable to work at, and miserable to do business with. Everyone was miserable - everyone, with the exception of the lucky "managers."

This is a worn out story that gets played out in business after business. It's as if most business owners view delegation as a vulgar four letter word that should be avoided. These owners are more than willing to take on responsibility themselves but refuse to delegate responsibility to their managers or front line employees. While there are several reasons for this, the result is the same: A company that absolutely sucks because of misplaced responsibilities. It's as if everyone in the organization is on a soccer field running after the ball with no one thinking of what the positions are, and who should be playing in them.

If you want to build a phenomenal company, you simply cannot operate like this. There are hundreds of research studies that demonstrate that the clearer a goal or task is the more likely that the goal or task will be accomplished. While the numbers vary from across research studies, it's common to see more than a 150% improvement of goal attainment and task completion.

So how can you drive this type of clarity and performance to build a phenomenal company?

The solution is as straightforward as it is simple. It all comes down to:

1. Getting clear on the essential results that your business needs (revenue, profit, efficiency, etc…)
2. Getting clear on the positions that will be responsible for those results
3. Getting clear on the people who will accept the responsibilities and produce the results

While this is straightforward and simple, don't let the simplicity fool you. Also, don't assume that others simply "get" what their responsibility is. Remember, your goal is clarity of needed results and determining who'll be responsible for getting those results.

While there are many ways you can go about getting clear on results and responsibilities, I've found that going through the following four-step process is the easiest and quickest way to get you up and running with the least amount of complexity.

GETTING CLARITY ON RESULTS AND RESPONSIBILITIES

Step 1: List All Required Results

If you want to free yourself from low efficiency and high misery, the first order of business is to stop for a moment and go big picture on the essential results that your business must produce. That is, take out a sheet of paper and write down all of the results that must be produced by your company.

Don't be fooled by the simplicity of this exercise. If you do it right, you'll find that it's much more difficult than it sounds. In fact, if you're like most owners, it will be more difficult for you to decide which results are essential and which are supporting the essential. For this exercise, focus only on the essential and be ruthless in removing the clutter (they're nothing more than "busy work.")

Step 2: Create an Organization Chart

Creating an organization chart for your company is beneficial in two key ways.

First and foremost, an organization chart clearly defines who reports to whom and helps you identify accountability leaks within your company. One major killer of productivity in any company is blurred lines of accountability. Usually this happens when a person reports to more than one manager. The problem with a person that reports to more than one manager is that no one really knows what that person does. Have you ever seen or experienced the following?

Boss 1: Kate, did you get my project done on Friday?

Kate: No, I am sorry, I was working on a project for Boss 2

Later on that day...

Boss 2: Kate did you get my project done on Friday?

Kate: No, I am sorry, I was working on a project for Boss 1

The point here is that when you have employees reporting to multiple bosses, it almost always fails because lines of responsibility are not clearly defined and no one really knows what the person is working on (for Boss 1 or Boss 2). There's also a burden on the employee of deciding which projects get priority (typically it's the easiest or the one they want to work on).

Creating an organization chart clears all this up for both you and for your managers. Be sure that if you discover reporting relationships where an employee has two bosses, you change it immediately.

The second benefit is that with an org chart you can clearly identify who'll be responsible for getting which essential results accomplished in the company. As an owner or manager, the responsibility ultimately falls to you to achieve all the essential results, but remember – you don't have the responsibility for actually producing those results, just getting them.

Step 3: Create Position Agreements

Ever since you started your business you've probably been told that you should have job descriptions for each employee and that you should leave them vague enough to give yourself some room should the job change. While this conventional wisdom sounds logical, I have yet to see hollow and vague job descriptions work in real life.

Typically job descriptions describe positions in broad language that's not very objective or measurable. Think about it. How exactly can you objectively measure "helpfulness" or "assisting" or "supporting." You can't. Because of this, most job descriptions are in no way connected to the real day-to-day functions of the position, and their results aren't measured. Your employees don't really know exactly what's expected of them, which results matter, or what responsibilities they have.

When it comes time to review the employee, the review is more like a political process than a real objective view of how that person is helping the business. Their grade is too often dependant on how well you or your manager likes the person, not necessarily what he or she actually produces for the company.

To prevent this, use position agreements.

Position agreements are very different than job descriptions because they clearly explain exactly what the employee does, how to do it, what the result should be and the standards that are associated in producing that result.

While you can arrange a position agreement any way you like, it should contain at least the following sections: Position title, who that position reports to, the main result the position produces, reporting positions, critical result areas, position standards, and signatures.

Step 4: Have Your Employees Review and Sign for the Responsibilities

Once you have your positions, results, and responsibilities sorted, and you have an org chart that shows how it all fits together, it's time to communicate your expectations clearly to your employees.

This step is not to simply sit someone down and quickly review their position agreement. It's meant to really take your time, schedule a one-on-one, sit-down meeting with each employee and explain in detail exactly what result he or she is hired to produce, how they'll be measured in producing that result, and what standards they must follow.

Use this meeting to clarify with them the finer points of the agreement and to communicate what's essential and important. The goal here is for both you and the employee to be clear on what their responsibilities are and what objective results they're expected to produce.

Once you've reviewed all areas of the position agreement, both you and the employee should sign your name on the agreement. Your signature is there to promise the employee that you'll provide the training, tools and standards so they can handle their responsibilities and achieve your agreed upon results. The employee signs the agreement, which indicates they accept the accountabilities of the position and agree to produce the listed results.

GETTING STARTED

I know that we've covered a lot in this chapter, but there's really only one take-home message here.

If you want to build a phenomenal company, you must get the players on your team playing in their positions and producing the results that the business needs. No more following the ball. No more just looking and acting busy. You must create clarity regarding what's most important for each position through a position agreement. That position agreement is your version of Coach Pug's wristbands.

The great news is that you can download templates for this 4-step process at: coalmarch.com/build.

Here you'll find templates for identifying the essential results of your business, org chart samples, and position agreement templates; just about everything it takes to build a winning team.

CHAPTER SUMMARY AND ACTION CHECKLIST

- Don't expect your employees to know what to do right off the bat. Tell them exactly what you expect of them, otherwise they'll busy themselves with tasks that don't have value.
- Delegate. You cannot focus on the operation of your overall system if you don't hand the smaller ones over to your employees.
- Make an organizational chart. You should know what basic results your company requires and who is responsible for delivering those results. Share the chart with your employees.
- Put those responsibilities into a position agreement. Make sure your employees fully understand their responsibilities. This will give them the direction they need to produce more valuable work.
- Go to coalmarch.com/build to download the resources for this chapter

"If you can't measure it, you can't improve it."

- Peter Drucker

Chapter 9

Step 4:

Define the Lines

Imagine, for a moment, that one day while you're at work you get an email from the local radio station notifying you that you're the grand prize winner of a contest – one that a friend entered you into without you even knowing it.

The grand prize is an all inclusive, VIP Super Bowl prize package that comes complete with first row seats to the big game, first class airfare to the city where the game will be played, 5- star hotel accommodations while you're in town, limo rides to and from the game, and even backstage passes for the halftime show entertainment. No expense was spared for this grand prize and you just hit the jackpot.

Finally, after months of anticipation and excitement, the day arrives for you to begin your very own VIP Super Bowl experience. Your first class flight to the city is amazing, your 5-star hotel accommodations could not be better, and you're driven like a boss to the big game in your very own stretch Escalade limo.

As you take your VIP seat on the front row, the excitement in the stadium could not be higher. The sound meter that measures noise in the stadium is off the charts. People all around you are screaming, laughing, and consuming more adult beverages than they should. You and your friends are in on the fun and are enjoying champagne and caviar, compliments of the big grand prize.

As you look onto the football field you notice something very odd. It's just one big grassy field, nothing else. There are no out-of-bounds lines, there are no yard line markers, and there are no end zone markers either.

Just before the kickoff, an official announces that for tonight's big game that there would be no out of bounds and they would not track the yardage on each play. Instead, they'd observe each play in real time and then tell the players if they did "good" or "bad." If the play was "good" the team with the ball could keep the ball, if the play was "bad" then the opposing team would get the ball.

On the first play after the kickoff, the quarterback throws a screen pass to a receiver that isn't even on the grass field. Instead, the receiver runs behind the opposing team's bench and catches the pass. The officials call the play good since there is no out of bounds. Many fans boo and scoff, but the game goes on in this disorganized and chaotic fashion.

The very next play a running back breaks through the defensive line and runs the ball all the way down the field into the end zone for a touchdown. The crowd goes completely bananas. The jumbotron starts flashing touchdown, people are laughing, screaming and some are even crying because of the incredible scoring play.

As the excitement over the play settles down, the most paradoxical thing happens. The officials decide that for this game they would not show the score until the game was over. Their rationale was that if one of the teams knew that they were losing, they might feel bad about themselves. It's better to wait until the end to show the score, rather than making a team feel bad.

And so the game proceeds with no out-of-bound lines, no yard line markers, and no score displayed on the jumbotron.

The players on the field begin to think, what's the point? Why should I risk getting pummeled by a 350lb lineman to score a touchdown that doesn't get posted on the scoreboard? We might already be winning anyway.

The audience in the stadium and the millions of people watching on television begin asking the same question as the players. "What's the point of this game? Is this even a game at all?" The game has evolved into being nothing more than a bunch of players running around in pads who don't know what's going on any more than the spectators do.

All of the excitement that once filled the stadium is now gone. There's no passion. There's no excitement. There are no players pushing to get just one more yard. There is no longer any drama to the game. In fact, this is no longer a game at all. It's pointless, boring, and... just like working at a company that doesn't track and report numbers to its employees.

THE INNATE DESIRE TO WIN

While the above example is outlandish, can you imagine if NFL games were really played like this? How many people do you think would watch them? How many people would play them? How much money do you think the NFL would generate? How would that compare to what the NFL generates now? The answers to these questions are obvious.

Most people want to be on and part of a winning team. People want to feel successful because being successful feels good. In fact, winning feels so good that some people (also known as football players) are willing to be pummeled by 350lb lineman just to get that feeling of success.

In 2007, the Harvard Business Review (HBR) released a research study on high employee performance, and what they found confirms that we, as humans, are more productive and more successful when we're actively engaged in a game. Below is a small excerpt from the findings of that study:

"For nearly 15 years, we have been studying the psychological experiences and the performance of people doing complex work inside organizations. Early on, we realized that a central driver of creative, productive performance was the quality of a person's inner work life—the mix of emotions, motivations, and perceptions over the course of a workday. How happy workers feel; how motivated they are by an intrinsic interest in the work; how positively they view their organization, their management, their team, their work, and themselves—all these combine either to push them to higher levels of achievement or to drag them down...

..Inner work life drives performance; in turn, good performance, which depends on consistent progress, enhances inner work life. We call this the progress loop; it reveals the potential for self-reinforcing benefits. " - Inner Work Life: Understanding the Subtext of Business Performance, HBR 2007

The study discovered (not surprisingly) that a key driver of maximum employee performance is how they feel about themselves, their work, their company, and their managers. If you get it right, the employee enters what the HBR termed a "progress loop" in which the employee wins, feels good, wins again, feels even better, and the progress loop ensues.

Likewise, employee performance suffers dramatically when they feel bad about themselves, their work, their company, and their managers. If you get it wrong the employee will enter a negative loop in which the employee feels bad, performs poorly, feels worse, performs worse, and so on and so forth.

LINES AND MEASUREMENT

So what does this study have to do with building a phenomenal company? Everything.

A service company, in many ways, is just like a football team. That's to say, your "product" is the performance output of your people. If your people don't operate or are not utilized at their peak, your product, the output of your people, is inferior to other companies that know how to extract peak performance from their employees.

The point is that if you want to build a phenomenal service company, then you must learn how to get people to work as hard as they possibly can. That is, you must create progress loops in which your people win so that they feel good about themselves. If they feel good about themselves (e.g. they score a touchdown) then they perform at a higher level and the progress loop ensues.

Ask yourself, "Is it possible to create progress loops if you have your employees playing a game with no out-of-bound lines and no yard line markers?" The answer, of course, is obvious: it's absolutely impossible, no way.

Some owners and managers try to get around this by giving arbitrary positive feedback, or complementing their staff, but these attempts to create a progress loop are ineffective at best and downright manipulative at worst.

Most people want to be engaged in and play a game that helps them feel good about themselves and ultimately be successful. Most people are motivated by progress because progress, in and of itself, is a sign that they're making a difference and that they're successful. When an employee can honestly and objectively say to himself, "I played a game and I won," a progress loop is possible.

Without defining the lines in your company and measuring performance, it's absolutely impossible to get the best performance from your people because they never have the opportunity to be successful. Even if they are successful, it's not recognized or noticed. The lack of measurement and the feedback it provides strips the employee of the emotional boost that occurs when they have a win for the company.

Think about the Super Bowl scenario described previously. When people are placed in a game without data on how they're performing and there are no goals to achieve, people lose interest. There's no passion. There's no drama. There's no motivation to work as hard as possible or to stretch as a person. Ultimately there's no game, therefore there's nothing to succeed at and there's nothing to feel good about. This is a sure recipe for employee mediocrity and dissatisfaction.

If you take nothing else away from this chapter, take this one idea:

Your job as an owner or manager is to create a game that is measured so that employees can win.

Don't misunderstand the point that I am making here. I'm not suggesting that you create games based on the "everyone gets a trophy" principle.

What I am saying is that if you own or manage a service company, your primary product is your people. If you want your people to perform at their absolute peak, then you must build progress loops in which the employee feels good about themselves. If you want to build progress loops, then you must create a game, complete with tracking, that allows the employees to win and create the positive loop.

Just like in a football game, it's the lines and the measurement that add all of the excitement and drama to the game. It's the measurement that provides the framework for the players to succeed. It's the lines and measurement that motivates people to do their best. It's the lines and measurement that makes people feel good and win. It's the lines and measurement that makes goals easy to identify, work towards, and ultimately achieve.

DEFINING YOUR OWN LINES
FOR MAXIMUM PERFORMANCE

Luckily, defining the lines at your company to create performance loops is not very difficult, so long as you don't overcomplicate it. Overcomplicating the creation of a game that's worth playing is probably the main reason that most owners and managers never attempt to create a game worth playing.

Supreme Court Justice Oliver Wendell Holmes once said, "For the simplicity that lies this side of complexity, I would not give a fig, but for the simplicity that lies on the other side of complexity, I would give my life."

What he meant by this quote is that usually in life there are simple answers to problems; however, to fully grasp the simplicity of those answers, you must understand and pass through the complexity in order to fully comprehend the simple. For example, most people know and have seen Einstein's E=mc2 but only a small fraction of people comprehend how profound this equation really is. E=mc2 ties together three disparate parts of nature: energy, light, and mass. To fully understand and appreciate the simplicity of this equation, you must first take a trip through the complex. And most of us don't have the mathematical and physics background to do this, so the simplicity eludes us.

But for you, the good news is that if you created your organization chart and position agreements from the previous chapter, you've already passed through the complex and are now ready for the simple. That is, you've already created the game and defined the lines. Now all you need to do is provide the feedback.

The following is a simple 3-step process you can use to get started creating your own progress loops so that you can maximize the performance of your people and ultimately your company.

Step 1: Review Your Org Chart

In chapter 8, we went through the process of identifying exactly what results your company needs and the positions that will have the responsibility for producing those results.

To start the process of creating your own game, go through each position on your org chart and identify the top 3 highest priority results that each position needs to bring to your company.

For a CEO it might be revenue, profit, and company value. For a front-line technician it could be production, sales, and customer experience. The point here is to ensure that all positions have at least three key result areas and that those results can be measurable objectively.

The key word here is objectively. If you find that one of the result areas is not measurable, then replace it or shift it so that it can be objectively measured. You cannot measure "positive" or "helpful" so don't track these things and don't put them into your game.

The goal is to identify only three essential result areas for each position. For most positions, there will be more than three result areas the position is responsible for. That's OK. Just pick the top three. If you have a position that doesn't have three key result areas, then look at the tasks associated with creating a result and make the task one of the three essential result areas.

This step identifies how to make a touchdown and defines the boundaries of each position so that you create the game that starts the progress loop for each employee.

Step 2: Build a Tracking Mechanism

Once you've identified the three key result areas for each position, now it's time to build your scoring system.

This is the step that many owners and managers don't follow through with. This is usually due to one of two problems:

1. They don't have the right systems in place to capture good data.
2. They don't have the technical expertise to create the proper reporting.

For a moment, I want you to imagine what a 20 percent increase in productivity would do for your company. How much more profit would you make if you achieved a 20 percent productivity increase? What would that mean to you in actual dollars? What about a 30 to 40 percent increase?

I ask this question because too often I hear business owners and managers object: "I don't know how to create a tracking system," or "I cannot get my office staff to track those numbers".

To these folks I can almost guarantee that if they run the numbers and calculate the amount of money that's leaking out due to a lack of people playing a game, they'll buy the software, fire the employees that refuse to track, and do whatever's necessary to overcome these obstacles. Why? Because the payoff is tremendous.

Step 3: Automate It (if You Can) and Push It

Last year, one of my service companies invested in a reporting tool that generates key metrics for each position in our company and "pushes" the top three result areas in the form of a text or email to every employee. This one small change completely transformed our company.

Employees began to look forward to the reports before they were released. Systems that seemed never to gain traction fixed themselves because now when something wasn't quite right, the data was pushed immediately to the employee who could fix it. Sales went up, customer experience scores went up, and even employee satisfaction went up.

While there is much more to this story that I could share, the main point is that it's very important that once you establish the top three result areas for each position, that you report on progress frequently and consistently. Otherwise you'll have a game like our imaginary Super Bowl that's simply not worth playing.

If, for whatever reason, you cannot automate your reporting, don't let that stop you from creating the game. When we first started as a company, we created simple spreadsheets and manually updated them until we could figure out a way to automate them. The goal here is to give your employees timely, appropriate, and actionable feedback so that they can know when they're winning, know when and where they need to improve, and always know what their goals are. Automation has nothing to do with this. No excuses.

ONE WORD OF CAUTION

Before we close this chapter, I want to leave you with one word of caution. I've seen some companies take on the project of measuring everything in their business but completely miss the point of measuring in the first place. It's as if they completely miss that there's a big difference between information and insight.

As you go through the process of defining your own game by drawing lines and establishing touchdown zones, don't lose sight that the goal is always to improve employee performance. Improving employee performance does in fact require data, but it also requires insight to what that data means. Improving employee performance requires that you actually do something with the data so that both you and your team ultimately win the game.

CHAPTER SUMMARY AND ACTION CHECKLIST

- Take advantage of our innate desire to win by setting goals for your employees. Meeting goals makes them feel good, feeling good about their work makes them more productive, and more productive employees mean a stronger business overall.

- Without goals or progress markers, your employees won't know what their hard work is for. This discourages forward momentum and hurts your business.

- Goals are meaningless without a way to track them. Tracking progress keeps everyone on the same page and allows employees to adjust their course if they're not on track to meeting their goals.

- Automate the tracking if you can.

- Go to coalmarch.com/build to download the resources for this chapter.

"I believe in standardizing automobiles. I do not believe in standardizing human beings. Standardization is a great peril which threatens American culture."

- Albert Einstein

Chapter 10

Step 5:

Standardize the Essential

Right now as you are reading this book, there are United States Air Force aircraft airborne all over the world. Without fail, the Air Force flies missions 24 hours a day, 365 days a year. These missions involve transport, surveillance, refueling, bombing, and air-to-air fighting. Some of these missions are for training, some are operational, while others happen in actual combat.

Take just a moment to grasp how complex it is to maintain an air platform all across the world. There are time zone issues, country-specific issues, aircraft issues, maintenance issues, pilot training issues, medical issues, mission issues, and the list goes on and on.

There are literally thousands of aircraft located in hundreds of locations all over the world. The number of aircraft in operation changes everyday, the locations of those aircraft change every hour, and the people who operate those aircraft change every single hour, too. There's no such thing as a day off, and the missions never stop.

Each part of the air platform has its own set of unique needs that must be managed on a daily basis. The aircraft must get fueled, the pilots must be trained, the missions must be coordinated with other countries, etc, etc… and yet the Air Force manages to consistently fulfill its mission successfully on a global scale.

To manage the scale and the complexity of this behemoth of an organization, the Air Force relies heavily on standardization and systems. It has to. How else can you deploy aircraft, aircrew, support personnel, parts, etc, on a global scale and keep up with it all? By what other means could so many moving parts be coordinated to carry out the mission of the Air Force so consistently and so effectively?

As a pilot, I'm dependent on systems, standards, and checklists when I'm in the air. When flying, there are countless life or death decisions that must be made quickly and correctly. The systems, standards, and checklists all work together to provide a structure that ensures that the majority of my decisions will be accurate and the best method to address any given situation is executed. I have procedures for starting engines and for shutting them down. I have standards for how to land the airplane, to judge if an approach is good, and whether or not to take an aircraft airborne. Heck, I even have procedures that dictate when I can go to the bathroom!

Although Hollywood would like you to believe that a good pilot has "the right stuff" and "is a loose cannon," most pilots will tell you that the great pilots are the ones that know their systems, procedures, and checklists extremely well. Indeed, the vast majority of aircraft accidents attributed to human error are almost always a result of a pilot not following a standardized procedure or a checklist. Likewise, in just about every heroic recovery of a disabled aircraft, you'll find that the pilot followed a predefined procedure to safely land the aircraft.

THE VALUE OF USING A STRUCTURED SYSTEM

So what exactly is a system? More importantly, what do systems have to do with building a phenomenal service company? Aren't you supposed to be unique and stand out of the crowd? Aren't you supposed to do things "differently" as a business?

Michael Gerber, the author of the E-Myth™ book series, gave one of the clearest definitions of a system that I've ever read. He states:

> *"A system is a set of things, actions, ideas, and information that interact with each other, and in so doing, alter other systems."*

This means that, in reality, everything is a system. The Air Force, your company, your family, the way you tie your shoes, the way you brush your teeth, and so on and so forth. Whether we are aware of them or not, in the real world we use systems every day to provide predictable, consistent, and effective results.

A system doesn't have to be complicated or confusing. A system just needs to have the following 4 basic components:

Procedures. A system must have a structured approach to provide a specific result. Procedures provide both the how-to aspect of the system along with the order. If your system has no procedures and no order, then it is not a system at all. Procedures allow the system to be performed in a manner that produces consistent, repeatable results.

Reliable Result. A system must provide a reliable, desired result. If the system cannot produce your desired result consistently, then you either don't have a system, or you have a broken one. In either case, it's time to go back to the drawing board.

Quantification. A system must be quantifiable to indicate if you achieved your objective or not. With quantification you can evaluate the effectiveness of your system along with the effects that system modifications have on desired results.

Standards. Any system must have performance standards. The idea is that, with standards, there is a common way to approach problems and tasks. The real value that standards provide is the ability to improve. Standards allow you to test new ideas, methods and technologies in your system and empirically validate their effectiveness.

The point here is that systems, standards, and procedures provide a structure to help you provide effective, consistent and phenomenal results. Once you have identified a quantifiable desired result, all that's needed are standards and procedures, and you have a system.

HIGHLY SUCCESSFUL ORGANIZATIONS USE SYSTEMS

While I don't believe that you will find this term defined in an academic journal or a college textbook, my wife suffers terribly from a disorder that I've come to term as OCDD. That is, obsessive compulsive Disney disorder.

Every year my wife wants to go to Disney, and to her it really is the happiest place on earth. She loves Disney so much that when our 15-year wedding anniversary came up, I gave her the offer of a lifetime. To avoid yet another vacation at Disney, I told her, "Honey, as you know our 15-year anniversary is coming up and to celebrate such a milestone in our marriage I'm willing to fly us anywhere in the world to celebrate it." Nothing was off the table. London, New York, San Franciso; literally I was willing to go anywhere in the world with her. Where did we go? Yup, it was Disney. Only this time it was without kids. Talk about weird.

While there's nothing about Disney that I particularly don't like,

I also don't want to spend every vacation of my adult life there either. Don't get me wrong, I love standing in line in a place that's hotter than the surface of the sun all the while listening to my kids complain over just about everything. It's wonderful.

While Disney, as an experience, has somewhat lost its luster for me, as an organization it's quite the rock star. Disney makes movies, Disney provides vacation excursions, Disney owns network channels, Disney has a cruise line, Disney has its own clothing line, and let's not forget that Disney has the most famous theme parks in (and all over) the world.

If you've ever been to Disney with children or a spouse who've lost their minds then you've no doubt attended what Disney calls a "character meal". A character meal is nothing more than a heist in which Disney provides you with limited meal options and the "experience" of meeting a few Disney characters.

Over the years of attending these character meals and exhausting more hard earned dollars than I'd like to admit, I've observed that the program follows essentially the same pattern. That is:

1. You are seated.
2. You are given a menu with only three meal options.
3. You are told that the characters are going to come out and that you should get your cameras ready.
4. The characters come out and you get your photo to share on social media (so that everyone knows that you're at Disney and

that you're crazy for participating in the heist).

5. The characters lead a parade of kids around the restaurant.
6. You pay the bill and falsely believe that you will never do it again.

I bring this up because I've observed this same pattern at multiple character meals, in multiple parks, at multiple Disney restaurants. This pattern is Disney's system for giving your kids a little entertainment while providing you with a "quality dining experience".

The most amazing thing about the character meal system is that it works extremely well for the target audience. How do I know? Well, the character meal is one of my kids' most favorite activities and my wife insists that we attend at least one of these dining experiences each time we go to Disney.

While this is a silly example of just how highly effective one of Disney's systems is, the reality is that Disney is built on a collection of highly effective systems that get results. There are systems for allowing people into the parks, systems to keep the park clean, systems for keeping patrons safe, systems for entertaining kids while they wait in line, systems for just about everything that the company provides.

Why would Disney invest so heavily into standardization, systems, and procedures?

SYSTEMS ALLOW YOU TO MAKE REAL PROGRESS

The day-to-day grind and the reality of owning and operating a business is that you're constantly bombarded with problems and issues to resolve. Each day is filled with resolving customer issues, financial issues, marketing issues, and, of course, employee issues.

Having problems as a service company is really not a problem at all, it's really just business as usual. However, a serious and more insidious problem is that most service companies continue to have the same problems over and over again. It's as if these companies have plateaued in their ability to make progress as an organization and for whatever reason they can't seem to make any real progress in key areas of their companies.

One of the most common recurring problems I see that holds most service companies back is their inability to see that the real problem is a lack of great systems.

Most weak owners and managers unconscionably blame other people for the problems in their business, not their own inability to build and execute systems. These weak owners and managers assume that most problems stem not from a lack of systems, but from people simply not doing their job or from an overbearing customer. So these owners and managers fire the employee or they fire the customer, only to have the same problem pop up again a month later.

Once again they think to themselves, "here's another 'bad' person."

What never occurs to these weak owners and managers is that, in reality, they don't have a people problem, they have a systems problem. Instead of looking inward, they look outward. Instead of spending the time to think through how they can solve the problem over the long term, they take the easy route and blame others (because it's easier and requires much less work).

These same owners and managers will protest: "I can't get this guy to perform," or "my managers will not hold others accountable," or "this person has a bad attitude," or "that person just isn't motivated." The reality is that there are systems for all of those problems and unless systems are developed and followed, the same problems will happen over and over again and your business will stop making progress.

In short, systems are the catalyst for real progress in your company and it's impossible to improve without them. That's why Disney and every other great company is into systems while bad to mediocre companies are not.

HOW TO GET STARTED BUILDING SYSTEMS IN YOUR COMPANY

When you have a systems-driven company, you have a platform in which you can improve month after month and year after year. Over time, with the ability to make consistent progress, your company snowballs to become not just a good company, but a phenomenal company.

So just how do you create a systems company? How do you standardize your operations? What's the best way to install systems into your company?

Step 1: Start at the Front Lines

Oftentimes, business owners will not take the time to create standardized systems for their companies because they are completely enamoured with the day-to-day operations of the business. Ms. Smith has an issue that you must deal with. Someone didn't show up for work today and now you're the one who has to get the work done. You just realized that the bathroom is out of paper towels and you need to go to the store to get more. The list is ongoing and neverending. It's the front line work and the small tasks of the company that are constantly dominating your time and your energy.

If you take anything from this chapter, take this.

If you're ever going to have a phenomenal company, you must start by making time and having energy to build your company.

So priority number one is to get yourself out of the day-to-day operations of the business as much as possible so that you can start creating the systems that drive phenomenal results at your company.

The easiest way for you to free up more time and have more energy to build your company is to first build out the systems, checklists, and procedures that your front line needs to do their work. The more you document what needs to be done and make it clear to your front line people, the less they'll need you during daily operations.

This one step creates the most time for you as an owner or manager. Your goal is to spend less time in operations and more time in building your company.

Step 2: Create a Checklist

The simplest step to get you started in building out your systems and procedures is to develop a simple checklist of tasks that must be done for each department.

A checklist is a powerful tool because it answers two basic, time consuming questions that can derail your efforts to create more time for you to build the business:

1. What should I be doing?
2. When should I do it?

While this step may seem so simple that you'll be tempted to skip it, don't. Years ago, when I went through the process of standardizing the systems of my first service company, I started with the office. At that time, we were what most southern people would term a "hot mess."

We had cash flow issues, we had customer issues, we had technicians fighting with the office, we had accounts receivable problems, we had accounts payable problems (because usually we didn't have any cash).

After implementing a simple office checklist, the most amazing thing happened. The majority of our problems simply went away. The technicians were nicer to the office because there were fewer mistakes being made, our customer service scores went up because fewer mistakes were being made, and our cash flow problem went away because fewer mistakes were being made.

The point here is that the checklist made all of the difference. The checklist provided the reference point to ensure that everything got done when it was supposed to get done.

Step 3: Create Procedures for Each Item on the Checklist

Once you have a checklist complete for a department, the next step is to clearly define each item on the checklist. What I mean by "clearly define" is to make a spelled-out, written procedure on how to accomplish each task on the checklist.

You should write these procedures so that someone off the street could read your procedures and operate your checklist without any assistance required from you or anyone else.

Think of your procedures as an expanded form of your checklist.

If an employee doesn't know how to do something, he or she can simply look at the expanded version of the checklist (your procedure) and easily understand how to accomplish that item on the checklist.

Step 4: Create a System for Validating Your System

No system is complete without a system for validating the results. While it may seem overwhelming to implement a standardized checklist for each department with expanded procedures, the reality is that's the easy part. The more difficult part is to ensure that these checklists are being accomplished on time and according to procedures.

As you might guess, a simple validation system can make certain the checklists are being used and followed according to procedures. While it's impossible for me to tell you how to create a validation system for each one of your checklists as the work required varies wildly from industry to industry, the point is to make sure that you have a system that follows up and substantiates that the systems you put into place are being used and done correctly. At the end of the day, you must inspect what you expect.

Your validation system doesn't need to be complicated or sophisticated. Your validation system can be as simple as a weekly task on your calendar to review checklists for completion and the work produced from the checklist for accuracy.

Step 5: Repeat for Every Position in the Company

Once you go through this process for a single department in your company, you've done all of the heavy lifting you need for standardizing your critical systems. But just like learning how to ride a bike, the first time you go through this process, it's going to be slow and you are going to make mistakes. It's going to take time and a lot of effort. Don't get discouraged.

If you stick with the process and follow one department all of the way through with its checklist, backed up with procedures and a system for validation, you'll have a platform that you can use to do the same in every other area of your business. Your next department is going to go faster, and the department after that even faster.

Make sure that you continue this process until you have systems and procedures in place for every department and every position. Doing so will empower you and your people to create a highly profitable, phenomenal company that customers and vendors love doing business with and where employees love to work.

CHAPTER SUMMARY AND ACTION CHECKLIST

- Systems are made of four key elements: procedures, reliable results, quantification, and standards.
- Using a system allows you to see if the system or the person operating within it is flawed, and adjust as necessary. They are the source of growth and progress in your company.
- A phenomenal company won't build itself — you have to remove yourself from the day-to-day operations of your business if you expect to have the time and energy to build systems that work.
- Create checklists for yourself first, then for each position in your company. Then develop a way to validate that your employees are following those checklists.
- Go to coalmarch.com/build to download the resources for this chapter

"Whatever you do in life, surround yourself with smart people who'll argue with you."

- John Wooden

Chapter 11

Step 6:

Attract the Right People

If you could choose between being a fox or a hedgehog which would you be?

No doubt, if there was ever an animal popularity contest between a fox and a hedgehog, the fox would win, bar none. For centuries the fox has been the main character in many folktales, books, and movies. The fox is sleek, beautiful, and has cunning intelligence. This thoughtful and resourceful animal can survive and even thrive in many diverse habitats including forests, grasslands, mountains, suburban areas, and even large urban communities.

The disesteemed hedgehog however doesn't enjoy the rock star reputation of the fox. In fact, there's nothing beautiful, cunning, or special about the hedgehog at all. A small spiny rodent, the hedgehog is a slow, quiet animal that aimlessly plods along from one destination to the next. You don't see movies like *The Fantastic Mr. Hedgehog* or read books like *The Hedgehog and the Hound*. Hedgehogs don't even get a supporting role in folk tales like "The Gingerbread Man".

So, which would you choose? Would you rather be a rock star fox or an unassuming, slow, and quiet hedgehog? If you're like most people, the fox is an obvious choice. Who doesn't want to be smart, beautiful, and popular?

In 700 B.C. a famous Greek poet and philosopher, Archilochus, asked himself this very same question. After considering this question for many years, Archilochus wrote a now famous parable that summarized his conclusion:

"The fox knows many things, but the hedgehog knows one big thing." - Archilochus

In the parable, the fox employs strategy after cunning strategy to try to catch and ultimately kill the hedgehog, who sneaks, pounces, races, and plays dead. And every time, the fox slinks away defeated, with a nose full of spines. Teeming with wit and clever ideas, the fox never learns that the hedgehog knows how to do one thing perfectly: defend itself.

In 1953, philosopher Isaiah Berlin took this parable and applied it to the modern world. Jim Collins further developed the idea of a fox versus a hedgehog in his classic 2001 book, *Good to Great*. According to Collins, organizations are more likely to succeed if they focus on one thing, and do it well. By doing so, they can beat their competitors and become truly great businesses.

Like most parables, the parable of the fox and the hedgehog has multiple deep meanings. And while there's certainly merit to doing one thing well, I want to extend both Berlin's and Collins' interpretation to your skills as a service company owner or manager – because the ramifications of this parable are significant.

THE MASTER SKILL

At the risk of you not reading the remainder of this book, I'm going to let you in on the most clandestine fact of owning and managing a service company. In fact, just like the parable, if you can fully grasp and comprehend the idea of having and developing one master skill as an owner or manager, then you don't actually need to do anything else in this book. That doesn't mean that it doesn't need to be done, it just means that you don't have to do it.

Just like the hedgehog, if you can develop and master this one key skill, it will pay you dividends as an owner or manager for the rest of your life. And just like the skill of hard work can help you be successful in any area of life, this skill, when learned, will help you be successful in all areas of business.

Before I divulge this secret skill, I want to take just a moment to review a couple of key concepts because it's critical that you fully comprehend their significance before we discuss the master skill.

Concept number one is:

As a service company, <u>your people</u> are the service.

That's to say, it's not the service that really matters in your service company. What's a service? It's essentially an inanimate object or thing that has no value until it's put into the hands of a person who understands how to provide it to a customer.

What would you care more about if you met with a financial planner, the data or the interpretation of that data? What do you care more about when you visit your doctor for a routine physical, the blood work or your doctor's analysis of your bloodwork?

The point here is that while systems, procedures, and checklists are all absolutely essential and necessary to provide a consistent service, they're all means, not ends. These tools are created for one purpose only – not to actually perform your service or satisfy your customers, but to enable your people to perform your service and satisfy your customers.

Concept number two is:

You can control things, but you cannot control people.

That is to say, in an ideal world you can create a checklist, write procedures for that checklist, and hand it off to a person who would execute it consistently and flawlessly every single time. The reality, though, is that in the real world, things simply don't work that way.

When you're dealing with people, both as customers and employees, things constantly change. Customers' preferences change. Customers' needs change. Sometimes moment to moment. There are certain situations in which following a checklist might be a dumb thing to do, and there may be instances when deviating from a procedure is absolutely the right call for that specific time and situation.

The point here is that most service company owners and managers have it all wrong. They believe, incorrectly, that they're in the financial planning business, or in the health care business, or in the home services business, but nothing could be further from the truth.

The truth is that the technicians working in these businesses are in the financial planning business, or in the healthcare business, or in the home services business, but the owners of these businesses are not.

As a service company owner or manager, you're not in the service business, you're in the people business.

This is the real secret of being a highly successful service company owner or manager. Just like a hedgehog, you must understand that you only need to know one big thing to be successful, and this is it. Your job is to find, attract, and retain really good people, because that's your business. Everything, and I do mean everything, else in your company can be delegated to the right people. Your marketing, your sales, your service, and even your culture can all be delegated to the right person.

If you take nothing else from this chapter – heck, if you take nothing else from this entire book – take this: at the end of the day, there's a causal relationship between the success of your company and the company that you keep in your business. Your primary responsibility, which cannot be delegated, is to attract, empower, and retain the very best people to your business. If you can do that one thing extremely well, then all other problems and issues will eventually go away. That's your hedgehog. That's your "one big thing."

IT ALL STARTS WITH OPTIONS

So just how do you as a service company owner or manager get out of the business of service and into the business of people? How do you take on the responsibility of finding and empowering the right people to put their boots on the ground serving your customers? The answer is marketing.

Years ago, when I started my first service company, I probably made every mistake that a business owner could make. In our second year of operation, I was very much still working in the business and I hadn't worked myself out of the field yet. Just like the two technicians that worked for me, each morning I'd come in, get everyone what they needed, follow up on customer calls, and then I'd go out and work on a route for the remainder of the day.

That year, our company experienced explosive growth. Like most business owners, every waking moment had me focusing my energies on growing the company because I knew that we needed to make more money as a business if we were going to survive. Luckily, my efforts were paying off, but as it turns out, I wasn't quite as smart as I thought I was.

While I'd put in countless hours of study, planning, and execution of our marketing and sales strategy, I hadn't given much thought to how we'd actually get all of the new work done. As we grew, I just assumed that I'd place a few ads on Craigslist and hire new employees as needed.

Boy, was I *really* wrong.

Two weeks into July, the two other technicians and I were working 14-hours a day and we were still not able to handle all of the service requests that were coming in. I'd anticipated growth, but I was completely blindsided by the demand for our services. To make matters worse, I couldn't turn off my marketing, as the majority of my leads were coming from web searches. I didn't have one single ad posted for technician positions at the company. Why would I? Just two weeks ago we were just fine.

But now as July unfolded, I was in a serious bind. I didn't have enough people on staff to handle customer demand, and our service quality was suffering because we were working 14-hour days and most Saturdays. To add insult to injury I had no one in the pipeline to even interview, much less hire, and even if I did, I didn't have time to interview them.

That summer, I ended up hiring two technicians, even though I knew before I even hired them that I'd eventually fire them. I was so desperate for bodies that I'd hire anyone with the ability to speak and drive a truck. Just as I predicted, both of these newly hired employees didn't last ninety days because they simply were not a good fit for our company.

Had I put just a fraction of the time I put into my marketing and sales plan into my staffing and recruiting plan, I would've never found myself in that dire of a situation. This mistake cost me business, lots of frustration, and a hit on our company's reputation.

RECRUITING IS REALLY MARKETING WITH DIFFERENT CLOTHES ON

How do you go about marketing your business to potential customers? Do you wait until you need customers before you start marketing? Do you coordinate your marketing with the needs of your customers? That is, if you're a seasonal service company, do you adjust your marketing campaigns based on when customers are most likely to be receptive to your services? How much time do you spend on the marketing and sales aspect of your business?

If you're like most service company owners and managers, you're probably pretty good at marketing and sales. There's no doubt that sales are the lifeblood of your business, and to grow as a company, you must know your customer and their needs better than your competitors. Also, like most successful service companies, you probably also market year-round as you always have room to take on more customers.

The point here is that most service companies are reasonably good at customer acquisition through marketing and sales. Most companies understand that if, for whatever reason, the leads stop, over the long term that spells doom for their businesses. Knowing this, service company owners place a high degree of importance on the marketing and sales of their services because it's what pays the bills and keeps them growing.

But, as I learned the hard way, there's a lot more to growing a service company than being a really good marketer. To be truly successful you must also have systems to attract good people. This is where most service companies get into trouble.

For a moment, I want you to imagine a three-legged stool. A three-legged stool can only stand if all three legs are firmly in place and all three are of equal length. The three-legged stool is a perfect metaphor for what it takes to win as a service company because your success depends on three key abilities. These are:

1. Your ability to generate leads.
2. Your ability to create and execute highly effective systems.
3. Your ability to attract, empower and retain the right people to your team.

If you're like most service companies, you tend to focus more on one leg of the stool while excluding others. This is like trying to sit on a three-legged stool with different length legs. At best, it's very uncomfortable to sit on, and at worst, it will not stand at all.

The fact is that all three abilities must be present in your company, but the reality is that generating leads and creating systems can be delegated. You, and only you, get to decide who will be on your team. Attracting and building the right team is the master skill for any great leader or manager.

GETTING STARTED

I have great news when it comes to attracting the best potential employees to your company: if you already know how to attract potential customers to your business – that is you know how to generate leads – then you already know how to attract the right people to your business.

I cannot emphasize this enough: attracting the right people to your business is the same as attracting potential customers to your business. If you know marketing, then this process is going to look very familiar to you.

Step 1: Get Crystal Clear on Who You Want

Just like in any marketing campaign, the first step of attracting the right people to your business is to figure out who the "right" people are. While I'm in no position to tell you who's right for your company, there are a few things I'll share that I look for in potential employees for my companies:

1. **I like people who have a passion for something.** It doesn't have to be our company, and it doesn't have to be our service, but it must be something. Runners, bikers, political junkies, it really doesn't matter. The point is that they care about something. If you find someone who doesn't really have any hobbies, they have little passion and they probably won't be a high performer in your company.

2. **I like people who have had a struggle.** This is not a sadistic fetish of mine. The fact is, business is all about struggle and overcoming problems. If you have someone sitting in front of you who hasn't been battle-tested either as a child or an adult, you don't know how this person is going to respond when you'll need him or her most. Pass on them. It's not worth the risk.

3. **I like people who know how to work.** I don't think that I've ever sat in front of a potential employee who didn't tell me that they were a hard worker. In fact, it's pretty much useless to even talk about being a hard worker with a potential employee. A much better approach is to look for hard work in their background. What were their grades in college? Has this person ever had a hard manual labor job? Did they wait tables in high school/college? You get the idea.

Step 2: Create a Conversion Funnel

Just as in marketing, you need to understand the needs of your target potential employees and build funnels to move them along the process of applying for a position at your company.

In the downloadable PDF for this chapter, I'll walk you through exactly how to do this, but for now, know that the funnel is essentially broken into three sections and you should know and understand the numbers you can measure at each section.

INDEED
ZIP RECRUITER
CRAIGSLIST
WEBSITE

JOB AD TRAFFIC

CLICK THROUGH
AD VIEW

ACTION

ACTION
FORM FILL
PHONE CALL

CONVERSION

APPLICATION
SUBMITTED

1. **Top of the funnel** - This is essentially all of the traffic that your job ads generate. This could be measured based on ad traffic to your website or to your job listings.

2. **Middle of the funnel** - At this point in the funnel, your goal is to get the potential employee to engage with your company. Whether it's through learning more on your website, calling your company to ask questions, or completing a contact form to learn more, the idea is to get the potential employee to take some sort of action that gets them get closer to eventually submitting an application.

3. **Bottom of the funnel** - This is the conversion part of the funnel, where a person transitions from being interested in your company to actually applying for a position. Again, as in marketing, you should know the conversion rate of the traffic and leads that apply to your company.

Step 3: Set Goals

Again, just like in marketing, you'll want to set goals for your recruiting efforts in two major categories:

1. **Applicant generation** - Set goals for the number of applicants that your recruiting system generates. You want to be in a position to put the right people in the right positions as you grow and you can also upgrade employees if necessary. By tracking the applicant generation metric you can learn which

recruiting channels work the best and which ads resonate with your target applicant.

2. **Qualified applicant conversion** - Another important statistic to track as part of your recruiting system is the number of qualified applicants that are eligible to be hired. Knowing this number allows you to see which channels are most effective and where you should focus your recruiting dollars.

Step 4: Launch Your Campaigns

Finally, once you have your conversion funnel set up and you've established goals for the performance of your recruiting system, the last and final thing that you should focus on is how to get as many people into your recruiting funnel as possible. Of course there are all sorts of campaigns to do this, but the point is to have your conversion infrastructure in place so that you don't waste money generating unqualified applicants to your company.

THE REAL WORK OF A SERVICE COMPANY OWNER AND MANAGER

There's much more to know about how to attract, empower, and retain the right people, and more details will be covered in the downloadable PDF. The point of this chapter is not to set the specific strategies for your recruitment efforts but to help you understand this simple but critical concept:

As a service company owner or manager, even if you're doing the technical work of the business, you're not in the service business. You're in the people business.

As such, your primary responsibility as a service company owner and manager is deciding who you'll surround yourself with. This responsibility cannot be delegated to anyone else.

To be truly successful as a service company owner, you must give as much emphasis to building the recruiting and people systems of your business as the marketing and sales systems. Why? Because it takes people to deliver the service you're selling. Without attracting the right people and providing them the systems to be truly effective, you have no real service to sell.

Just like the fox and the hedgehog, there's a big difference between knowing a lot of things and knowing one big thing. Your one big thing as a service company owner or manager is your understanding that you're in the people business, first and foremost, because that's the key to everything else in your service company.

CHAPTER SUMMARY AND ACTION CHECKLIST

- As a service company, your people are your service.
- You are not in the service business, you are in the people business. Your role is not to be a technical expert, but to build a solid team of quality people.
- Recruiting employees is just as important as marketing to customers. The wrong hiring decision can hinder your growth and negatively impact your bottom line.
- Go to coalmarch.com/build to download the resources for this chapter.

"The only thing worse than training your employees and having them leave is not training them and having them stay."

- Henry Ford

Chapter 12

Step 7:

Build Your Training Program

With four small children at home, by far my most favorite holiday is Christmas. I enjoy the holiday even more now as an adult than as a kid because for me there's nothing more fun than to watch how excited my kids get as they open presents from Santa.

As you can imagine, starting and growing a business is a very time and energy consuming activity that can require herculean efforts to keep going. A few years ago, closing in on Christmas, I was in the midst of one of these efforts when my wife just happened to mention to me that Santa needed to put together some toys for Christmas morning.

While I'm sure that you've probably never done this, I procrastinated my Santa duties until Christmas Eve night. Once the kids got to bed, Mrs. Claus started bringing box after box of toys that Donnie the Elf had to get assembled before the next morning. There were dollhouses, bicycles, playhouses, and countless other smaller toys that required some sort of assembly prior to use.

Dutifully, I worked my way through the boxes and got almost all of the toys assembled. The last toy that needed my attention was a large, green, John Deere tractor for my son Blake. This tractor was impressive. It had a front loader, a cab, a backhoe, and even stabilizer legs. While most people would see this spectacular and sophisticated toy tractor as the perfect gift for a little boy, at 1:30 a.m. on what was now Christmas morning, I was thinking that maybe Mrs. Claus should have opted for a more basic model.

Nonetheless, I began the task of assembling this tractor, that with all of its lavish attachments was sure to please any young boy. If you've ever stayed up on Christmas Eve night to assemble toys, you probably already know that reading directions and assembling toys after midnight can be a little stressful. After struggling through a few tricky steps, I glanced at the clock to see that it was now 3:43 a.m. I knew I needed to wrap up the assembly before the kids got up at 5:00 a.m., (don't ask, I've tried to move this wake-up time ahead for several years) so I quickly finished putting the wheels on the tractor and called it a morning.

It felt like I'd just laid my head on the pillow when my kids burst into our bedroom at 5:00 a.m. on the dot to start the Christmas morning activities. We had a grand time that morning opening presents and my kids were elated with all of the assembled toys that Santa left by the tree that night.

The elation of the morning soon faded later in the day, when my son Blake asked if he could take his new John Deere tractor out for a spin in the driveway. As he began driving the tractor down the hill of our driveway, I could tell immediately that something was amiss. The large rear right wheel of the tractor began to wobble violently back and forth. I called out to my son to stop but he couldn't hear me over the roar of the tractor tires.

Eventually the wobbly tire came completely off the axle and rolled down the driveway right into the garage.

Being quick on my feet, I told Blake that one of Santa's elves must have missed something when he assembled the tractor. It certainly wasn't his neglectful Dad that's for sure. After looking over the wheel and the axle of the toy tractor, I immediately identified the problem. Santa simply forgot to install the linchpin to hold the wheel on the axle. During the assembly, at 3:43 a.m. Christmas morning, I managed to get the wheel on the axle, but didn't manage to install the linchpin that secured the wheel into place.

TRAINING IS THE LINCHPIN OF YOUR COMPANY

So what does the misfortune of a little boy on a half-baked tractor have to do with building a phenomenal company? Well let's just say that they have more in common than you might think.

A linchpin is a very small pin that fastens to an axle that prevents the wheel from sliding off. If you were to see a linchpin in real life, you'd think that it was quite unimpressive. A linchpin is nothing more than a small metal pin, usually with a ring attached to one end, for easy installation and removal.

Yet while the linchpin appears small and simple, its role in the wheel assembly is the key element that holds the entire complicated structure together.

Your business, just like a wheel assembly, is no doubt a complicated structure. There are moving parts and each part affects the other parts. There are schedule commitments, sales commitments, invoices to be sent out, discussions that need to happen, phone calls to be returned, and dozens of other activities.

At the hub of all this complexity and activity are two very critical things: your people and your systems. As we mentioned in the last chapter, if you want to have a phenomenal company, you must understand the concept that a phenomenal service company is built on phenomenal people. If you want to have phenomenal people, then there is no substitute for the requirement that you attract, develop, and retain phenomenal people.

Training Is the Linchpin for Developing and Retaining Phenomenal People.

Training is the one activity that, if done consistently, affects every critical number in your business. Oftentimes, especially in a service company, almost all problems can be traced back to a training issue. When you really start digging into these problems, you'll find that sales, customer service, and collections are not really the problem; training is.

SPEND MORE TO EARN MORE PROFIT

What if I told you there's a guaranteed way to make your business extremely profitable and easy to manage, and one that customers love doing business with? What if I guaranteed that I could increase your profit by 24% with only a $1,500 investment and the solution is both easy and fast? Furthermore, I assure you that I will not be using any techniques from the Charles Ponzi or Bernie Madoff playbook. Would you believe that I could fulfill such a guarantee?

As we covered earlier in the book, as a service company you are in the people business. Yes, you provide a service and yes, people purchase your services, but when you peel all the layers back, at the end of the day, you're in the people business.

People account for the largest expense on your profit and loss statement. This means that any performance improvements, even if they're only minor ones, have a massive impact on the bottom line of your business. Research proves over and over again that training and developing your people is the linchpin to empowering them – and empowered employees are good for business. Let's review the research.

HAPPY EMPLOYEES PRODUCE MORE

Like it or not, millennials are in the workforce and they, probably more than any generation, understand the competitiveness and insecurity of today's work environment. Technology is changing on a daily basis and employer loyalty is a thing of the past. Understandably, millennials place high value on training and the opportunities for advancement because they want to survive the new realities of the workplace.

PricewaterhouseCoopers recently conducted a survey in which the following question was asked of millennials:

"What are the characteristics that make an organization attractive to you?"

The top two answers for this question were:

1. Opportunities for career progression
2. Excellent training/development programs

An IBM study shows this same trend, only in reverse. IBM found that employees who feel that they cannot reach their career goals or develop within their career are 12 times more likely to leave the company.

TRAINING AND RETRAINING CURRENT EMPLOYEES COSTS A FRACTION OF HIRING NEW ONES

So what? What's the problem with employee turnover? Isn't a little turnover good for your organization? As a service company that's dependent on people to perform a quality service, not hardly. In service companies, employee turnover is often a catastrophic event considering the amount of time involved in changing employees.

Think about it. When you lose an employee, who picks up the slack? That's to say, how much time do you end up paying in overtime wages? When you lose an employee, how much time does it take to recruit another one to replace him or her? When you lose an employee, how much time does it take to get the new employee to a point that he or she can start producing revenue for your business?

This is a critical point because oftentimes, most business owners and managers just look at the hard cost of turning over an employee. That is, they only look at the hard costs that show up on the profit and loss statement, like recruiting costs. But this is not even close to representing the real cost of the change, because no costs are attributed to time loss. And as you already know, time is the most expensive element in a service company. When you factor time back into the cost of losing the employee, what you'll find is that the true cost of turning over an employee is more than triple the hard costs.

A meta-analysis research study on the actual costs of hiring a new employee showed that on average the cost of hiring was typically about 30% of the position's salary. That means if you're hiring for a position that pays $40,000, you can expect to incur $12,000 in costs to hire that person.

Training an existing employee, however, usually doesn't cost more than a few hundred dollars, and takes far less time than hiring a new one. Even if replacing one employee doesn't sound that bad, consider that replacing three employees equals an entire annual salary of a new employee, yet you get no real gains for your business.

It doesn't take a rocket scientist or math teacher to figure out that the recruitment and training costs of new hires are exponentially higher than the costs of simply training your existing employees extremely well.

These research studies clearly demonstrate how expensive employee turnover is, so the insight to take away here is clear: if you want to boost profit, reduce turnover. To reduce turnover, train your employees. Trained employees are happier, more productive, and less likely to leave your company.

TRAINED EMPLOYEES EARN MORE MONEY WITH LESS TIME

Another perk of spending more on training your employees is the causal relationship between training and employee utilization (how much employees can get done in a given time frame). Cornerstone research completed a study on over 400 service companies and found that:

> "Companies that put a priority on employee development make median revenue of $169,100 per employee while companies that don't make $82,800."

While the actual median dollars found in this research study is impressive, what's more impressive is the insight that companies who make employee development and training a priority more than double the efficiency of companies that don't. That is, they are able to do more, much more, with fewer people.

If you think this is too good to be true, a different study conducted by ADP of 2500 businesses concluded that companies that offer thorough training had more than twice the amount of income per employee over firms that offered less training. Same conclusion.

The research is clear that highly profitable service companies maximize income per employee through focusing on effective employee training and development programs.

IT'S LEARNING, NOT TRAINING

Maybe this doesn't happen to you, but sometimes this happens to me. Have you ever given a presentation and then had someone ask a question that's so basic to what you were just speaking about you realize that this person didn't understand a single thing you said?

I ask that question because it's important to grasp that the purpose of employee training is learning, not training. Training is a means to learning, not something that you do by just checking the box.

When you were in high school or college, did you ever sit through any lectures in which you were physically present in the class but mentally you were completely checked out? Do you think that's possible when your employees "train" at your company?

I mention this because it's important to realize that as you begin to invest time and money into your training systems, you should keep in mind the big picture goal. The goal is learning. Pretty presentations and elaborate workbooks, while nice, don't guarantee learning.

Be sure that as you build your training systems, you validate the ends and not the means. That is to say, be sure that your training systems validate that learning actually happened.

You can do this through exams or on-the-job sign-offs, but no matter what, make sure that you verify that learning actually took place. Otherwise, just like the mental vacations you took in high school and college, your employees could physically accomplish the means because they're being "trained," but totally miss the ends because they learned nothing.

EXCUSE OR RESPONSIBILITY?

While most business owners and managers fundamentally understand the idea that employee training is good for their companies, when it comes to implementing an employee development and training program, most produce a half-baked system that simply fails to get the job done.

I've observed that most service companies have some variation of the "ride with Joe for a couple weeks" training program. While there's nothing easier than abdicating the responsibility of training your employees to someone else, it backfires over the long term.

First of all, the "ride with Joe" training system is completely unscalable and dependent on Joe's mood and what he remembers when he's riding with the new employee. The other problem is that it communicates indirectly to the employee that they're not worth your investment of time and money to train them properly.

Predictably, the new employee begins to make mistakes. Unfortunately, what's equally predictable is the response from owners and managers. Instead of blaming themselves or the training system, these owners and managers blame the employee because "they should have known better."

A good test for "they should have known better" is if you can point to a specific training on the topic along with validation that the employee actually learned the subject matter. If this is the case, you're right. It's the employee's fault. My guess is that inadequate training is the root of the problem in over 90% of these instances.

The real problem is owners and managers using the excuse of "the employee should have known better" instead of acknowledging that it was a training system failure.

This trend of making excuses instead of accepting responsibility over time has dire consequences for your business. Your great employees will leave the company out of frustration, and you'll have to replace them with new, untrained employees. The net effect is that your entire staff will level down, not up.

HOW TO CREATE YOUR OWN TRAINING SYSTEMS

Luckily, building an effective training system is not complicated. I don't want to paint a picture of rainbow ponies and fields of gold when it comes to this. Like saving money or living on a budget, the process of building an effective training system is hard, but not complicated.

The key to building your own training system is to do it little by little, step by step. Below are four simple steps to get you started. The downloadable PDF for this chapter will walk you through the details of this process.

Step 1: Determine Needed Training Programs Based on Your Org Chart

Once you have your org chart, creating a training program for your service company is fairly straightforward. Personally, I like to create a training organization chart, as it clarifies and simplifies what training is required for your staff.

At the top of your training org chart, you should start with "All Team Member Training". This is the training required for all of your employees regardless of their position. General training such as sexual harassment, employee culture, and employee handbook training goes in this category. After that, separate your training into tracks depending on the position the employee is hired for.

Step 2: Complete All New Employee Training First

The second step of building a great training program is to complete one training track all the way through before you start on anything else. The idea is that you go completely through the process once and then after you have a section completely done, you then just replicate that on each block in each track until you completely fill out the training org chart.

The goal here is to define what training should be included in the block, develop the content for that block, write the validation for that block (whether it's exams, sign-offs, or a combination of the two), and then deploy that to your employees. Doing this for your All Team Member Training block does two things:

1. It gets everyone at the company on the same page with basic training for your company.
2. It allows you to get the issues and problems associated with your training program worked out before you invest a lot of time and money into the process.

Step 3: Create a Validation System for All New Employees

Years ago, an employee of a competitor contacted me because he was looking to make a change. He wanted to meet with me and explain some ideas he had on how he could help our company get to the next level. He spent almost thirty minutes explaining to me how much he knew and how valuable his knowledge was to a company like mine. He presented a plan to grow sales in a particular service line, and all but guaranteed that I could be completely hands-off while he grew that part of my business.

On the surface, this sounded like a good idea. We'd been struggling with that service line and quite frankly, I didn't feel that we were experts in the various technical aspects of the service. We did however, have basic training on this service line and we were learning more every day. As we learned more, we trained more.

Could this guy be the answer we needed? With all his knowledge and abilities, was he the key to finally succeeding with this service line? I was asking myself these questions as he was monologuing about all of the difficult jobs he'd handled over the years.

As he was talking, I decided it might be a good idea to be sure that what he was telling me was in line with what he actually knew. Surely a guy of his talent and caliber could pass a simple exam from a company completely new to this service line, because his knowledge of the service was more advanced than ours.

Once his pitch was done, I casually said, "this all sounds like a great idea. A salary request of $90k is more money than I'm currently making as an owner. Do you mind just taking a quick exam on this service just so I can see where you're at? It should be simple, as we're new to it. I just want to get your thoughts on our training for this service." He confidently agreed and he even offered to provide suggestions on how to improve the exam.

I'm not sure who was more shocked at his score, him or me. As it turned out, the talented employee of my competitor scored a 23% on an exam that all of my employees had already passed. Upon seeing the scores, I politely explained to him that he had a great deal working with his current company, and that I simply couldn't match the deal that he was currently getting.

Had I not had a training system that validated learning, I would've made an agonizing error. In this case, and countless other cases, simply validating learning made the difference between a major success and a major mistake.

It's important that any training you do is backed up with an exam or some mechanism that validates that the training was understood and, more importantly, retained. Without this, you may leave your employees with a false sense of value going into a customer's home, or soliciting other companies for a higher paying position.

Step 4: Repeat Until You Complete the Org Chart

The final step is to simply repeat what you've just accomplished for each block. I recommend that just like in steps 1-3, that you build your training system out track by track, rather than all at once. I've seen other business owners attempt to do it all at one time and fail. In many cases, it's simply too overwhelming to build an entire training system all at one time.

TRAINING IS THE LINCHPIN FOR A PHENOMENAL COMPANY

If you look at companies like Southwest Airlines or Chick-Fil-A, you'll find that they're big into training their employees. They understand that in order to have a phenomenal company, they must have phenomenal systems and phenomenal people to operate those systems.

If you take nothing else from this chapter, take this: training is the linchpin that positively (or negatively) affects all areas of your business, and if you want to build a phenomenal service company, you're going to have to build a phenomenal training system, because that's what empowers phenomenal people. Your role is to create the phenomenal training system to get the process started.

CHAPTER SUMMARY AND ACTION CHECKLIST

- Training makes the difference between a good employee and a great one.
- People value opportunities to learn and advance in their field. By offering position training you're building up better technicians and attracting driven, quality candidates.
- Trained employees are happier, and happier employees produce more and better results.
- Don't stop at training. Make sure your training system also validates that your employees are learning the material.
- Go to coalmarch.com/build to download the resources for this chapter

"**Your most unhappy customers are your greatest source of learning.**"

- **Bill Gates**

Chapter 13

Step 8:

Create Your Customer Loop

A few years ago, I decided that I was going to start going to the gym consistently. Up until then, my efforts to go to the gym regularly had totally and utterly failed. Each day I'd pack a gym bag and head off to work with the intention of working out before heading home. Then life would happen. My intended gym time after work would get hijacked by meetings that ran over, clients that called, and projects that needed to be done that day.

Finally, I realized that if I was going to make getting to the gym part of my daily routine, I'd have to go in the morning before my workday started. Once I made the change of going in the morning, the issue of consistency simply vanished.

My original intent in building the habit of going to the gym was to do something good for myself. No doubt, consistently working out would help me stay leaner, feel better, and ultimately be healthier. Building this habit has indeed delivered on my original intention, but it has also given me an unanticipated gift: entertainment.

If there ever was a laboratory for self-deception, it's not at a university, it's your local gym. Characters such as the guy that suffers from ILS (imaginary lat syndrome), Mr. Creepy Sweatpants, Too-tight Tee, Selfie Star, The Orange Lady, and Shorty Shorts have made the gym the perfect place to get in shape and become healthier, and also the perfect place for seeing the gap between reality and how people accept and deal with that reality.

SELF-DECEPTION AND YOUR COMPANY

More than 40% of one company's engineers said they're in the top 5% of their field. More than 90% of college professors say they do above-average work. One-quarter of high school seniors think they're in the top 1% in their ability to get along with other people. Three independent opinion polls forecasted Hillary Clinton's chances of winning the 2016 Presidential election at 70%, 89%, and even as high at 99%.

Do these numbers make sense to you? Is it really possible that 40% can be in the top 5%? If the definition of average is 50%, is it possible for 90% to be above 50%? How is it possible that three independent opinion polls completely missed the 2016 Presidential Election outcome? The answer is, quite simply, lies.

In college, whenever we discussed polls or surveys, my statistics professor would say "there are lies, there are damned lies, and then there are statistics." At the time, I thought this it was funny and just a joke. It took the 2016 Presidential Election between Donald Trump and Hillary Clinton for me to fully comprehend the real meaning of that phrase.

Polls and surveys of opinions, especially those collected by another person, can often represent an exercise in math rather than a representation of reality. That's because, when it comes to human behavior, we cannot escape one inconvenient truth:

People lie.

The point that my professor was making was that while, yes, you can collect statistics on opinion polls and surveys, the answers underlying those surveys are often lies. Respondents to polls and surveys respond with lies to help others feel good about themselves or to fit into what's considered socially acceptable.

While this may sting and may even seem a little dark, the cold hard truth is that we all lie. At best, we lie to ourselves, at worst we lie to others. I'm not talking about a deliberate, bold-faced lie or outlandish dishonesty. The lying that I'm talking about is far more difficult to detect and even more difficult to admit.

While it would certainly be an interesting topic to cover, it's well beyond the scope of this book to discuss the psychological and moral issues around the concept of why people lie and how often it happens. The research is clear that we all lie, and we lie consistently.

Why is it important that you know and understand this fact?

Because, just like Mr. Creepy Sweatpants, Too-tight Tee, Selfie Star, The Orange Lady and Shorty Shorts, your company is just as susceptible to self-deception because liars are running it! So I'm exaggerating a little here, but the fact is that, as humans, we all self-deceive because we don't have enough psychological strength to admit the truth and deal with the consequences that will follow. As a service company, your company is no different.

Think this is off-base? Ever hang on to an employee longer than you should, even though you knew it was time for them to go? What did you say to yourself? Ever continue investing in marketing that wasn't working because you didn't know what else to do? What did you say to yourself? Ever get feedback from a customer that deep down you knew was spot on, but you didn't do anything about it because acknowledging the problem meant a substantial change at your company that you didn't have the energy or know-how to tackle? What did you say to yourself?

I'm willing to bet that when you really peel back the layers of a company that's declining or has stopped growing, the very root of the problem is self-deception – either on the part of the owner, managers, or even worse, both.

And that's the problem. No company, just like no person, can ever change, grow, or get better if they self-deceive and are unwilling to solicit, accept, and deal with the truth. This very fact is what keeps psychologists in business and what provides entertainment in gyms all over the world.

INDIFFERENCE AND YOUR CUSTOMERS

For a moment, I want you to think about two specific customers that you've recently done business with.

For the first customer, I want you to think of one that causes the hair on the back of your neck to raise up. This person should be the biggest pain in the neck customer that you've ever had to deal with. This should be the customer who has complained to you the most. The customer who has made unreasonable demands. The customer who, for one reason or another, is never satisfied.

For the second customer, I want you to think of one that you really don't know very well other than they're no longer a customer. This customer was never a problem for you. They called you with a need, you gave them a service, and eventually they cancelled. This person was cordial and he or she never complained.

For a moment, I want you to picture both of these customers side-by-side. If you had to take back one of these customers, which would it be? Why?

If you're like most people, you're probably thinking that the customer who was nice to you but indifferent to your company is the better choice. If that's your choice, you're dead wrong.

Can you think of one major win that your company has had over the past five years? If so, what was that win? How long did it take you to overcome it? What drove you to the win in the first place?

There's a paradoxical relationship that exists in life between success and problems. On the one hand, we don't want problems. Dealing with problems is, by our own perception, problematic. Problems mean change, problems mean work, problems means stretching, problems mean awkward conversations and problems are hard.

On the other hand, it's problems that bring us to the point of changing to make things better. In fact, I'd argue that oftentimes it's not until a problem becomes almost unbearable that we become compelled to do anything to resolve it.

So while problems are "problematic," an undeniable fundamental truth is that it's only through problems that we develop as people and it's only through problems that we develop as companies. This means that fundamentally:

Avoiding problems is avoiding opportunities to get better.

If you don't know what your problems are, you're either not looking for problems (or opportunities) in your company or you're deceiving yourself by believing that those problems don't exist. Either way you're stuck in the mud and going nowhere fast.

We started this section with the question of which customer is worse to have. Undeniably, the indifferent customer is a much worse choice because you'll never learn about the problems you need to fix in order to get better. It's impossible to rise to an opportunity if you never know what the opportunity is.

When you think about it, in most cases, the most significant and positive changes that have occurred in your company happened as a response to a problem. Without the problem, there would never have been those positive and significant changes.

Your "problem" customers are nothing more than your opportunity customers. They'll tell you, without any effort on your part, what's wrong and what needs to be improved. They've already done the homework for you.

Years ago, I'll never forget hearing these words over and over from my team regarding the problem customers, "Donnie, we're dealing with 1% of our customers here. Is this really worth it? Do we really need to do this for the 1%?"

My answer in almost all cases was (and still is) emphatically yes.

Here's why:

Your 1% of problem customers make it wonderful for the other 99% to do business with you.

SELF-DECEPTION AND INDIFFERENCE

Sitting in an emergency room, Charley Howson explained:

> "I've had three children, and I'd rather give birth than go through anything like that again. It was sharp, as if I had swallowed acid, and I couldn't breathe. I was gasping, but just couldn't fill my lungs. I thought I was going to die."

Just hours earlier, Charley was going about her normal day cleaning her home when she decided that she was going to deep-clean her kitchen floor. Charley took ammonia from her cleaning cabinet and mixed it with boiling hot water and bleach.

What Charley didn't realize was that mixing ammonia and bleach together creates highly toxic and often fatal chlorine gas.

If there ever was a combination that could create chlorine gas in your company, it's undoubtedly the combination of company self-deception and indifference on the part of your customers. It's already hard to improve and stay competitive when you self-deceive; it's impossible when you don't know what's really going on in the minds of your customers.

GETTING PROACTIVE

As a company, it's not easy to get the time and attention of your customers. We're all overcommitted, overscheduled, and more importantly, overwhelmed. Never in the history of the world have we, as a society, been as highly educated and as overscheduled as we are today.

In previous generations, we focused on acquiring the basic resources such as food, water, and shelter. In modern societies, our scarcest resource is time. Time is so scarce that most people are willing to use disposable income on products or services to get more of it.

We're always on, always connected, and usually highly opinionated. In the past, our parents and grandparents only had one, maybe two choices for consuming a certain product or service. In today's world, that number is in the hundreds and thousands. In a matter of seconds, we can access a trove of data on all our options for a service and then rack and stack companies based on past customer experiences.

When your customers have so many commitments and so little time, you can't expect them to take the time to provide you with unsolicited feedback. It's not that they don't have opinions or feelings concerning your company, they most certainly do. It's simply that they don't have the time to communicate those back to you. In most cases, especially if you provide a service that the customer is not passionate about (or not at home for), the customer is completely indifferent as to who performs the service, as long as it gets done.

Ultimately, this means that as a company, simply waiting for customers to provide you with unsolicited feedback is analogous to watching grass grow. It will happen, but it will be very slow and in most cases you won't even recognize the feedback when it does come. If you're serious about improving as a company, then you must create systems that get in front of your customers, get their attention, and initiates feedback so that you can improve your customer experience.

CREATE A CUSTOMER LOOP

An effective customer loop is the solution for customer indifference and self-deception.

A customer loop is nothing more than a system for collecting as much unbiased data from your customers as possible, analyzing that data and then acting on it. The downloadable PDF for this chapter will walk you step by step through how to create your own customer loop, but in general, your loop should contain the following:

A Collection Platform

There's a dogma going around the service industry right now that says "you should collect feedback at the time you perform the service." The thought process behind this strategy is that if you collect the feedback at the time of service, you'll will get more favorable reviews and feedback. My question to you and those that are disciples of this dogma is:

Do you want to intentionally introduce deception into the feedback from your customers? If you're collecting feedback at the time of service, whether you realize it or not, you're influencing their response. Going back to the research, no customer is going to give you or anyone else honest feedback at the time of service because in many cases, it's not socially acceptable for them to be totally and completely honest to you or your people directly.

While collecting reviews at the time of service will indeed give you a flow of positive reviews, it will do nothing for exposing areas in which you can improve your service.

A better approach is to build a collection platform that allows your customers to speak as freely and as openly as possible without the pressure of lying to you. This can be done with a simple text or email survey, but the goal is to get as must truth as you possibly can from the customer.

A Measurement Platform

A second component of a customer loop is the ability to objectively measure key elements that drive customer engagement with your company. The idea is that you have a platform in which you can test over time the perceptions customers have of you and your company as you make changes.

Relying on third party websites such as Google or Yelp will not be enough to get the job done. Too often, only a "would you recommend" question is asked, and you also must cull through the comments to pick out any trends.

An easier way to do this is to use software that automatically scores and reports key customer perceptions over time so that you can identify trends and problem areas.

An Action Platform

While this may seem obvious, you'd probably be surprised (I certainly have been) at how many companies get great opportunities from their customers to improve, but they simply don't read or even engage with the feedback.

What's the point of collecting data if you're not willing to use the data for change?

For this part of the loop, make sure that you create a system that monitors customers' feedback consistently, and more importantly, actually does something with the data. At one of my service companies, when a survey comes in that's below a 9 (on a 10 point scale), we call the customer to find out why and what we can do to make it a 10.

DON'T BE GYM ENTERTAINMENT

An effective customer loop allows your company to be proactive about collecting real and true perceptions of your company from your customers so that you can get out of self-deception and into reality. Your goal is to see customer "problems" as real opportunities for you to provide a better service to your customers that ultimately allows you to grow and develop as a service company.

CHAPTER SUMMARY AND ACTION CHECKLIST

- Always be as honest as possible about the performance of your own company. Change a system that isn't working. Fire an employee who isn't a good fit.
- Your "worst" customers are your best sounding board. Don't take every positive review at face value. Customers who complain are handing you opportunities to reflect and improve with every complaint.
- Give your customers an easy way to provide feedback, and act on the feedback they give.
- Go to coalmarch.com/build to download the resources for this chapter.

"A body of men holding themselves accountable to nobody ought not to be trusted by anybody."

- Thomas Paine

Chapter 14

Step 9:

Create Your Accountability Loop

While I'm sure that this isn't the case in your family, in my family we have what I like to term "crazy." In my family, we don't reference crazy as a adjective as most others do, we reference crazy as a noun – as in a person. While you may not use crazy as a noun in your family, you know who these people are. These are the people whose lives, for whatever reason, function more like a reality TV show than normal life. These are the people who have drama almost every day, who are constantly offended by everyone, and should be avoided, if at all possible, because life is simpler and better with limited contact with crazy.

As in all families, our family has learned how to adapt to and deal with Crazy because that's what families do. Our philosophy is that while, yes that person is crazy, it's our crazy and crazy is family so we need to look out for crazy. We employ a number of effective strategies to stay out of and avoid the drama of crazy, but there are certain times of the year that we simply must be together.

A few years ago, our immediate family gathered with our extended family for the annual gorge fest, better known as Thanksgiving. We had turkey, stuffing, mashed potatoes, sweet potatoes, corn-bread, green beans, and all the other trimmings. Once we were finished with our meal, there was a round of desserts just waiting to put us in a carb-induced coma that would render us useless for the remainder of the day.

But that year, despite all of the great food, we had one serious problem. Our family absolutely loves pumpkin pie and Crazy was responsible for bringing it. The pumpkin pie Crazy brought was absolutely awful. I was the first one to notice it when I took my first bite and the expression on my face clearly communicated what I was thinking. My wife followed my look with one to me that I should not probably write about. I even tried feeding some to the dog. He wasn't having it either.

And so it went, with each member of our family discovering for themselves that the pumpkin pie tasted like cardboard. Like a true southern family, everyone pretended the pie was great while at the same time covertly hiding their pie trash in napkins or under other food on their plates..

Finally, Crazy had a piece of pie and exclaimed, "Oh no! I forgot to add the salt!" At that point, the entire family let out a collective sigh, no longer having to avoid the awkwardness of trying to pretend that we liked something that even our dog refused to eat. To this day, the pumpkin pie incident is still a favorite family story. Not because the pie was awful but because everyone was pretending it was great so as to not have drama with Crazy.

Pumpkin pie is by far one of my most favorite Thanksgiving desserts, and until the incident with Crazy, I never knew that salt was even one of the ingredients. It's ironic how one ingredient that's the opposite of sweet is actually the key ingredient that's needed to bring out the best combination of sweetness and the flavor of the pie.

In and of itself, salt is nothing special. Can you imagine eating a jar full of salt? Can you imagine drinking a glass of salty water? And yet, when combined with other things, salt becomes the catalyst that brings out the best in whatever it's combined with.

Salt can be used to enhance food, it can be used to clean things, it can be used to restore beauty, and can even be used to clear roads. Want to boil your eggs faster? Add salt to the water to boil it at a higher temperature so cooking time is reduced. Want to put out a grease fire? Throw salt on the fire to smother it. Want to brighten your curtains or fiber rugs? Wash them in salt and watch the colors brighten. Tired of feeling sore? Add a few handfuls of salt to your bath and soak in it for 10 minutes.

ACCOUNTABILITY IS THE SALT
OF YOUR COMPANY

A few years ago, I was asked to speak on the topic of maximizing profit through effective people management. The venue was an international conference with thousands of business owners from all over the world. Given the diversity of the audience and the broadness of my topic, I decided to focus on something that was common to everyone and absolutely essential for profit in all service companies.

I centered the presentation around the idea that research and history show a correlation between organizational accountability and organizational profitability. I detailed case study after case study of how companies with a culture of accountability outperform their peers in every measured category of business performance, especially profitability.

At the end of the presentation, a line of attendees formed to speak with me. I tried to answer as many questions as I could, but I couldn't help noticing a woman who, for whatever reason, kept allowing people to go in front of her. When I finally reached the end of the line, I asked her why.

She said that she had a "unique and specific" situation that was going to take some time to discuss. She was right. Over the next 20 minutes, this business owner began detailing how bad her office manager Debbie was.

Debbie showed up to work late. When the business owner tried to implement changes in the office, Debbie simply refused to make the changes and continued to do whatever she thought was best. Debbie was obviously resistant to change. Debbie liked to gossip about the other employees, and the woman speaking to me suspected that Debbie was gossiping about her. Debbie frequently had arguments with staff in the office and staff in the field. Debbie, Debbie, and more Debbie.

In short, her business was not growing, she was struggling, and in her mind, Debbie was public enemy #1. After a 20-minute rant about Debbie, I asked, "Is there anything else I need to know about Debbie?" Wrong move. That led to another 4-minute dissertation of the many character flaws and performance failings of Debbie. After two more rounds of my asking whether she wanted to add anything and her coming back with more, she finally said, "I think that's about it." I then summarized by saying that she believed her company was not growing or moving forward because Debbie was preventing it. She agreed with my summary and then the following conversation ensued:

Me: So what is your problem?

Owner: What do you mean what's my problem? Like I said, Debbie is doing all of these things and I don't know what to do. That's why I'm here. I'm looking for ideas on how to deal with Debbie.

Me: I understood what you said. That's why I repeated it back to you. I wanted you to know that I heard and understood you. So what is your problem?

Owner: Sir, I really don't understand what you're asking me. I apologize but I thought I made it very clear about all of the things that Debbie is doing and I thought you understood what I was asking.

Me: The problem isn't Debbie. The problem is you. Debbie is just fine. Debbie has a great life and does pretty much whatever she wants. Debbie doesn't have to change. Debbie doesn't have to worry about consequences. In short, Debbie is the one running your company, not you. I'm asking, is it a problem for you that she is?

Owner: Well, I am the owner and I am Debbie's boss.

Me: It certainly doesn't seem that way. You're asking me if there is anything you can do other than holding Debbie accountable for her actions because you're either afraid of her or you're not holding yourself accountable as her boss. Either way, it's your problem, not hers. So which is it? What's your problem. It sounds to me like she should've been gone long ago but you're unwilling to do it. That's not her problem. It's yours.

Owner: Oh? I could never fire Debbie. No, I won't do that.

If there ever was proverbial "salt" for your company, it's no doubt accountability. Accountability, like salt in a pumpkin pie, brings out the absolute best in your people. With accountability, everyone understands what's expected of them and they own the responsibility to make it happen. With accountability people care about results. With accountability, people work harder, stay later, and are more proactive. With accountability, people get results and that, in turn, creates results for the company.

On the other hand, a lack of accountability does the exact opposite. Without accountability no one really knows what results are expected. Without accountability, no one is held responsible for getting results. Without accountability, no one's willing to put in any extra effort because they simply don't care about the results as much. A lack of accountability, just like the lack of salt in a pumpkin pie, takes what would otherwise be a phenomenal and winning organization and debilitates it.

But don't go overboard with what I'm saying, as it's entirely and completely possible for the exact opposite to be true. While it's true that you need salt to bring out the best in your people, and the best in a pumpkin pie, it's possible to overdo it. Can you imagine a pie with four times the required salt?

Oftentimes, owners and managers understand the concept of accountability, but don't want the concept to apply to themselves, and will place their own accountabilities on others. That is, they add too much salt to their organization. They hold people accountable for results on which they have no authority or no direct impact. This is nothing more than the same problem in reverse. Instead of the employees not being accountable, the owners and managers are not holding themselves accountable, and eventually the employees get tired of dealing with an owner or manager who is all salt and no balance.

The reality is that most small to medium service companies have serious accountability problems and in most cases, accountability is the only thing preventing a good company from becoming a great company.

DO YOU HAVE AN ACCOUNTABILITY PROBLEM?

So why is accountability such a problem for small to medium sized service companies? Why is it that most service company owners and managers, like the owner at the presentation, will do almost anything to avoid holding others accountable even to the point of personal financial loss? Why is it that despite knowing, both intellectually and instinctively, that we have an accountability problem, do we avoid solving it?

The short answer to all of these questions is that accountability on the surface seems hard, especially in the short term, and is nearly impossible without an accountability loop.

It's All (Sort Of) in the Family

When your company is small, every day counts and every employee counts. If someone doesn't show up for work it's not just an inconvenience, it's a five-alarm catastrophe. When you're a small company someone not showing up for work can mean the difference between making money for the month or not. Many owners and managers walk on eggshells because they know they're extremely dependent on the few employees they do have and they can't survive without someone filling their shoes. These owners and managers feel vulnerable. This problem is exacerbated by the fact that most owners and managers only recruit when they have a real problem employee that they need to replace.

But when an issue of accountability comes up, it's much easier to not hold an employee accountable than it is to fire them, suffer as a business, start recruiting, conduct interviews, train someone new, only then to have the problem come up yet again a few months down the road. Given this reality, these owners and managers will allow employees to walk all over them and seldom draw a hard line of accountability. The risk is simply too high that the employee may leave and they'd be stuck going through the process of finding someone else.

Another common issue is the amount of involvement that owners and managers have with their employees when they're working right alongside of them. It's very natural and quite human to develop close relationships with those you work with day to day.

The problem is that many owners and managers take this very human tendency too far and don't hold employees accountable for fear of damaging the relationship that they have developed with them. It's as if these owners and managers are like the parents who'd rather be friends with their kids than be parents. And just like families where the parents are trying to be friends first, owners and managers who fail to be owners and managers first have dysfunctional businesses at best and employees who manipulate them at worst.

An unfortunate reality that I've personally observed in business is owners and managers being fiercely loyal to employees like Debbie. Instead of holding employees like this accountable, these owners endure years of missed deadlines and poor performance. For their loyalty, these owners and managers are rewarded by having the employee move on at their first opportunity to make more money at another company.

A Lack of Defined Results

Another huge impediment to accountability in a service company is that owners and managers haven't gone through the process of clearly defining the objective results needed by each position. Oftentimes owners and managers operate under the false assumption that employees understand what results they should be getting and will spontaneously and consistently produce them. This is simply not true.

Can you imagine telling a sales person to "just do your best to sell as much as you can" or telling an office manager to "get out the invoices when you get around to it" and then just expect them to do it? If you believe these tales, let me know when the Nigerian Prince who emailed you recently actually pays you off.

Without an objective result, there can be no objective accountability. You might get lucky and have an employee or two who's conscientious and who actually does a great job, but in most cases, what you'll find is that the lack of defined results is really code for "it is not my job."

Look no further than most government bureaucracies if you want to see what this looks like on a mass scale.

Responsibility Without Authority

Another barrier to accountability is requiring responsibility without providing authority.

Years ago, I worked with a service company that had reached $20 million in revenue but had flatlined for the previous 3 years. According to the owner, no one could figure out what to do next. When I met with his management team, I learned that nothing could be further from the truth. The management team knew exactly how to move forward. The problem was, they couldn't.

Whenever the owner "gave" responsibility to his managers for a project or decision, if he didn't agree with the decision, or if he had what he considered to be a better way of doing things, he'd immediately swoop in and change the decision. Without even realizing it, this owner was assuming all of the responsibilities and all of the accountabilities of the organization because no one had any authority without clearing all decisions through the owner. He didn't know it, but that owner was holding the whole organization back.

This resulted in an organization in which no one took accountability and no one was held responsible because the owner accepted it all. He was the bottleneck for all decisions because he trained his managers that they had no real authority and no real accountability. Over time, this decimated his culture and, ultimately, the results of his company.

The "Un" Follow Through

The final barrier to real accountability is what I like to call the "un" follow through. I've observed an interesting phenomena with owners and managers who have a lot of enthusiasm but not a lot of accountabillity when they realize that they need more salt in their organization. Typically the process goes like this:

1. Owner or manager attends a conference or visits another company and sees how well an accountable organization operates.
2. With all of the enthusiasm of a kid opening presents on Christmas morning, the owner or manager goes home and gets to work clearly defining what results are needed in the company.

3. The owner or manager communicates the results needed, then delegates out to the positions who will be responsible for those results.

4. The owner or manager moves on to a new project but never bothers creating a system to follow up on the results.

"Un" follow through is more common than you think, even among large service companies. The reality is that we're all so busy and life is moving so fast that you must create a system that reports results to you and to the position responsible for the results, along with adequate time to review the results together. Without a formal system of accountability, as time passes, both you and your employees will forget what the target result was and who was responsible for producing it. In most cases, the default is always you.

CREATING A CULTURE OF ACCOUNTABILITY

The details of how to create a culture of accountability are in this chapter's downloadable PDF. The point of this chapter is not to go through all of the details on how to create a culture of accountability, but to explain how critical accountability is to any great company, and how it's practically impossible to build a phenomenal organization without it.

In the PDF we're going to go through a simple 4-step process to get you started in putting some salt in your organization. Please note that while the steps are simple, implementation will no doubt test your integrity. The process to create an accountable culture is:

Step 1: Define the Results

I have great news. You've already completed this step. In Step 4 of the Build™ framework, you went through and defined the critical results for each position.

Getting clarity on what objective results your company needs is a gift for both you and your employees. With a clear benchmark to meet, your employees will feel good when they win. You won't need to pepper them with a hollow "good job" or "great effort."

Step 2: Assign the Responsibility

As in Step 1, if you've been doing the steps as you go through the book, Step 2 of creating a culture of accountability is already done for you. In Step 3 I had you create an organizational chart.

In this step, all you need to do is assign which position is responsible for which results. These results should be clearly spelled out on your position agreements and you should sit down with each employee to ensure that they fully understand the desired result.

Step 3: Systemize Accountability

You may be asking yourself, "Do I really need a system for accountability? I'm going to be looking at the results, isn't that enough?" The answer to that is unequivocally no. While I'm sure that you'll be looking at the results consistently, that doesn't mean that you'll consistently respond to the results the same way every time.

Your accountability loop should address this tendency and at a minimum, have the following components:

1. A clear definition of the desired result.
2. A clear line of who is responsible for creating the result.
3. An agreed-upon time that you and the employee will review the results.
4. A plan for what action happens next based on the results. This can range anywhere from termination to a promotion or raise. The point is that it's spelled out ahead of time so that both of you are very clear on the accountability and what occurs when results are achieved or not achieved.

Step 4: Exercise Integrity in the Moment

While this all may seem like a lot of work, it's actually quite easy in the long run. Bringing salt into your organization can be done without damaging relationships and without assailing anyone's character. In fact, if you do it right, an accountability conversation moves away from both of you and towards results.

The key to instilling accountability in any organization is shifting the conversation from a personal one to one that's focused on results. Rather than an open-ended conversation about what may or may not have been accomplished – a conversation that can lead to hard feelings or misunderstandings – you can point to the intended result, whether or not the employee attained that result, and how you can help them do better the next time.

I've had to let people go in my organization, and while I cannot say that all of them are friends, most of them are. It was nothing personal, and there was no drama, it just wasn't a good fit.

In the moment, when it's really time to make a hard decision, the most beneficial thing that you can do for both yourself and your employee is to exercise integrity. That is, to follow your accountability loop.

IT ALL STARTS WITH YOU

In the final analysis, no matter how you slice it, your company is nothing more than a reflection of you. If you're organized, your company will be organized. If you're dishonest, your company will be dishonest. If you're a person who values humor, your company will value humor.

Accountability works no differently. The quickest, most effective way to instill a culture of accountability into your company is to start with yourself. Hold yourself more accountable. Bring more salt to yourself and your organization will naturally follow.

True accountability, like salt, is the ingredient that brings out the best in everyone, including yourself, and will ultimately preserve your company in both good times and bad.

CHAPTER SUMMARY AND ACTION CHECKLIST

- Accountability brings out the best in your company.
- Lead by example. If you are accountable, your employees will see the importance and follow suit.
- Putting expectations and desired results in black and white will help your employees meet their targets and will make conversations about missed goals more straightforward.
- Don't undermine your employees' efforts by taking on their responsibilities. Hold them accountable for their wins and their failures.
- Don't forget to follow up. Monitor your employees' progress and have pre-determined steps for when goals are met or missed.
- Go to coalmarch.com/build to download the resources for this chapter

"I think frugality drives innovation, just like other constraints do. One of the only ways to get out of a tight box is to invent your way out."

- Jeff Bezos

Chapter 15

Step 10:
Engineer Progress

Many, many years ago, when my wife and I got married, we purchased a unique wedding gift for ourselves.

The gift was a simple plant that we used to decorate our concrete block wall college apartment. As college students, our decoration budget was very – and I do mean very – limited, and the plant changed the appearance of our apartment from looking like a prison cell to something resembling a very modest home.

Years after purchasing the plant, it became representative of us as a couple. The plant went with us to pilot training, the plant went with us to our first real jobs, the plant went into the first home we purchased, and the plant was placed in our first daughter's room right after she was born. In short, the plant, like our marriage, was the one constant in spite of all the life changes we were experiencing.

After ten years of having the plant, the leaves of the plant began to fall off and brown spots developed on the remaining ones. At first, I thought that maybe we were just not watering it enough or maybe it wasn't getting enough sunlight, but after three weeks of consistent watering and plenty of sun, I realized that the problem was much more serious than that.

I took the plant to a nursery to see if I could find someone that could tell me what was going on and if there was anything I could do to save it. I explained my concerns to the man behind the counter who, after taking a cursory look at the plant, asked me in an incredulous tone, "When was the last time you fed this plant?" Baffled by his question, I asked back, "What do you mean, when was the last time I fed it?"

For a decade, all we'd done was water the plant and place it where it could get plenty of sun. Not knowing anything about plants or keeping anything green and alive in general, it had never occurred to us that the plant needed food and nutrients. Now, years later, the plant had used up every bit of food and nutrients in the soil and no amount of sun or water was enough to sustain it.

After feeling like a total and complete doofus for not seeing the obvious, I purchased new soil and plant food and within two weeks the plant not only recovered but it looked as vibrant as the day when we'd gotten it a decade earlier. As it turned out, it wasn't the short-term stuff like sun and water that was killing the plant, it was the one long-term ingredient to a healthy plant: food and nutrients.

So what exactly does a plant that my wife and I almost killed have to do with innovation at your company? As it turns out, quite a bit.

No doubt, if you're phenomenal at the operations of your company that's great. If you're phenomenal in managing your business, that's wonderful. If you're phenomenal in executing strategy better than any of your competitors, congratulations. All these aspects of business are important and necessary, but like the plant with no nutrients in the soil, they are short-term in nature and they're not enough to sustain your company over the long haul.

When it comes to building a phenomenal company, being extremely good at what you do will bring many short-term successes. You can survive for years being great at operations, great at management, and even great at executing the most complex strategies, but the fact remains that just like a plant with no food, without innovation and progress, your business will eventually die. Innovation and progress are the "food" that sustains your business over the long-term.

In this chapter, we're going to review exactly how you can engineer innovation and progress into your business so that just like your other systems, you can consistently improve as a company. Some people, even some business owners, will claim that you can't systematize creativity or innovation. I'm here to tell you that this view is completely and totally false. Furthermore, it's even possible, if not predictable, to engineer innovation and progress right into your company. Companies such as Amazon and Google do it every day and so can you.

So just how can you engineer progress into your business? What system do you need to leverage the creativity of both your employees and customers to drive innovation at your company? As it is in most cases, it all starts with your soil.

A CULTURE OF INNOVATION

When was the last time you made a big mistake at your company? I'm not talking about missing a point during a meeting or mispronouncing or even forgetting an employee's name, I'm talking about a big business mistake. One that had operational consequences and financial consequences.

What was the mistake? When did you make it? How many people know about it at your company? How often do you make mistakes like this? Who exactly at your company knows that you made the mistake? Were you embarrassed by it? Are there any other leaders or managers at your company who make mistakes?

I ask these questions not because I want you to feel bad or to bring up the past. I'm asking them because these questions are a wonderful barometer of how innovation is going at your company. Honda's founder, Soichiro Honda, said it best when he said: "Success is 99% failure."

As paradoxical as this may sound, when you peel back what it means to have a company that embraces innovation and progress, what you really have is a company whose culture doesn't despise, but instead embraces mistakes and failure.

Research and my own personal experience show that time after time most organizations are not very good at accepting failure. In fact, most companies create systems to eliminate errors altogether. This is because most managers pray at the altar of results rather than innovation. A mistake to them is something that should be avoided, certainly not celebrated or encouraged.

A key obstacle that most owners and managers must overcome is a deeply ingrained aversion to failure. Research shows that for the majority of people their psyche registers pain more strongly than loss.

Creating a culture of innovation requires that you reframe failure as the required price of success. Please don't misunderstand what I'm saying. I'm not suggesting you throw caution to the wind and proclaim, "Look at us, we're failing, we're innovating!" Failing in and of itself is not innovation. But it is part of the process.

If you want to systematize innovation and progress at your company you must first create a culture where people feel safe failing. Create a culture that strikes a balance between performance and learning.

Equally important to embracing failure is to embracing curiosity.

Albert Einstein in his early years generally abhorred going to school. In fact, his Munich school teacher once quipped, "He will never amount to anything." But that all changed when he was 16 at Aarau High School, in Switzerland. There the teachers challenged him to nurture his curiosity and encouraged him to ask a lot of questions and express criticism.

It was this environment of questioning that allowed Albert to imagine things like what it would be like to ride a light beam – which later paved the way for his theory of relativity.

To create a culture that embraces progress and innovation, you need a combination of being curious, asking great questions, and being willing to fail when you try new things. Your goal is to create an environment where you, your managers, your employees, and even your customers are not only allowed, but encouraged, to ask lots and lots of questions. While this can be a challenge and even annoying, it's only through great questions that the critical thinking of innovation can be done.

THE INNOVATION MEETING
While I can't claim that I grew up on a farm, I did spend many summers working on a tobacco farm when I was young, even before

I could qualify for a worker's permit. Spending my summers with Mr. Tucker, the owner of the farm, taught me many things about work and life but there is one lesson that I'll never forget.

When I was 13, Mr. Tucker gave me what I considered to be, at that moment, the opportunity of a lifetime. For the three previous summers that I worked on his farm, I was assigned as a field worker. Field work on a tobacco farm is about as labor intensive and demanding as farm work gets. Even as I kid, I remember going home with many back and leg aches due to the physical exertion that was required of me in the field.

Now this year, Mr. Tucker told me that he needed me to drive the tractor to plow the fields. I was elated that Mr. Tucker would trust me with a tractor, and I must admit, I wasn't too sad to be leaving the field work either.

After about 30 minutes plowing my first field, Mr. Tucker came out to meet me on the tractor. Being a man of few words, I knew I must've been doing something wrong. With a little annoyance in his voice he asked, "Donnie Ray, where are you looking?" His question puzzled me. I mean, what the heck did that even mean? Of course I was looking straight ahead and also behind me so that I could make sure that my plow lines were straight. Only they weren't.

Mr. Tucker then had me stand up on the tractor to see the field more clearly. Once I stood up, I could see exactly why he had asked this question. My plow lines were not straight, but rather a series of small S-turns across the field. This, of course, wasted precious field space and over time would create larger S-turns in the field. Mr. Tucker then said something that I'll never forget: "Donnie Ray, you can't plow a straight line looking directly in front of you or looking behind yourself. Pick one tree across the field and drive directly to that tree."

Mr. Tucker's advice was by far the best advice I'd ever been given on how to plow a straight line. From that moment on, I was able to plow straight lines with no problem.

And so it is in business. You can't move forward as a company when you're constantly looking at what's behind you or at what's directly in front of you. Real progress as a company comes from the ability to see the tree across the field and remain focused on that.

What is that tree? Where exactly are you going? Can you maintain focus on that tree so that you don't simply S-turn as a business and waste precious time and resources?

The innovation meeting is designed to answer these very questions.

An innovation meeting is nothing more than a meeting in which you and your managers sit down and ask yourselves a series of questions such as:

1. How can we improve our customers' experience with our company?

2. Is there any new technology that we can leverage to help us be more efficient?

3. Knowing what we know now, are we repeating any old mistakes? What can we do to adjust?

4. How can we be more efficient?

5. What opportunities should we be thinking about?

This is just a list of sample questions and you should change them based on the needs of your business, but you get the idea. The sole focus of the meeting is to identify the tree across the field.

Your innovation meeting is your opportunity to stop, survey the field, and decide what tree your business is going to drive to next. When planning and conducting this meeting consider the following:

1. Have at least one innovation meeting annually. Schedule your innovation meeting well in advance and build the rest of your schedule around it. Otherwise, it's too easy to get caught up in the day to day and you'll never actually take the time to have the meeting.

2. Don't reverse order. A common mistake that many businesses make with innovation is that they launch into projects that are designed to implement the latest technology or "the next big thing" without actually questioning if they really need the technology. It's as if these companies are addicted to technology but never question the real usefulness or impact to their business. This is easy to do as a company especially if you

have persuasive and optimistic vendors. To prevent this, I recommend that before you evaluate any new technology in your business, you have your innovation meeting first. The idea is to identify the needs of the business first, then evaluate technology solutions to see if they can help. That way, when you see new and exciting technology, you'll see that technology through the lens of the needs of the business. Otherwise, you can end up spending your time on things that have little or no real impact on your business.

3. Don't go bleeding edge. While it may be tempting to jump at a brand new technology, I don't recommend it. When Bill Gates was CEO at Microsoft, he pioneered a concept that had never been considered before in the software development industry. Before the era of Microsoft, software developers would never think of shipping software with known bugs or shortcomings. Doing so would have meant disaster for those companies because their reputation was on the line. Bill Gates however had a different approach. At Microsoft, software was shipped whether it was bug free or not. Bill's philosophy was to ship the software and fix issues as they came up. As you can imagine, this created many problems and headaches for companies that were early adopters of Microsoft software. They were used as nothing short of unwitting software testers. Shipping new software with known issues and allowing customers to test the software is

common practice these days. With the speed at which companies must change, customers are used to test all of the features of newer technologies. The point here is don't be a pioneer when it comes to implementing newer technologies. Pioneers come back with arrows in their backs. Allow other companies to test and work the technology so that most issues are resolved before you implement it at your company. The reality is that if you live on the bleeding edge of technology, you are certainly going to bleed.

DON'T MISTAKE TECHNOLOGY FOR INNOVATION

When I was growing my first service company I was appalled by the lack of technology in my company's industry. With a software engineer's background, the industry as a whole seemed to be very behind in adopting technology and in my mind, it was costing me lots of money.

At that time, mobile technology was exploding in multiple industries, but for some reason the software providers in our industry hadn't caught on to the many efficiencies and benefits of using mobile units out in the field.

I decided that instead of waiting any longer on our software providers to catch up, that I'd just write our own mobile app instead. Gone were the days of paper tickets. Gone were the days of printing out route sheets. Gone were the days of paper map books. We were going to create our own app and be a company of the future, or so I thought.

I was going to write a mobile app that solved all of these problems, and I did. It eliminated all of the paper products we used, but it certainly didn't turn out as great as I thought it would.

First of all, it took me almost six months longer to write the app than anticipated. Secondly, now that I had a mobile app, that meant that I also had to support it. So when new bugs showed up, guess who had to fix it? When the server went down, guess who had to fix it? When a software that the app integrated with changed, guess who had to fix it?

Over time the mobile app became a huge distraction for me and for my company. There were new feature requests that had to be managed, there were the software bugs that had to be fixed, and let's not forget that the app could not integrate with our customer management system.

I'd lost sight of the bottom line: we were not a software development company. We were a home services company. The mobile app had nothing to do with our core business but consumed a large majority of our time.

Finally, one day I thought to look at the number of hours that the mobile app saved versus the number of hours we spent on support, maintenance, and development. As I glanced at the total column, I couldn't have been more disgusted. It was costing us on average 2-3 times more hours with the mobile app than the dumbed-down paper system that we were previously using.

On the surface, our mobile app seemed sexy and our company appeared to be extremely innovative. In reality, we just used more technology; the mobile app had no real bearing on actual operational performance.

Looking at the hours spent versus the benefits to the business, I realized that I had made a serious error. I had assumed that technology would lead to innovation and performance improvements in the business. I was wrong.

I'm telling this story because I learned a valuable lesson from the mobile app gaffe that I believe every owner and manager should understand:

Technology is not innovation.

Before you decide to implement any new technology, be sure that from a business effectiveness and performance perspective that the technology is a win. Otherwise, you risk wasting a lot of time and money for something that may look cool, but doesn't really move the mark.

ENGINEERING PROGRESS AT YOUR SERVICE COMPANY

In the accompanying PDF for this book, we'll detail exactly how you can systematize and engineer progress and innovation into your company and your culture. Here we're going to briefly describe the process but please keep in mind that there are many more steps behind this process that makes it all work.

Step 1: Schedule an Annual Innovation Meeting

If you're a small company, invite key customers and even other business friends to the meeting. If you're a larger company, all of your managers should attend as well as anyone else at your company that's really good at asking basic questions.

Step 2: Schedule an Annual Technology Review Meeting

Be sure that you do this after your innovation meeting so that you avoid the temptation to implement technologies that don't offer real or desired innovation.

Step 3: Inventory and Review Innovation at Your Company Annually

The final step is to measure innovation so that you can make better innovation decisions. That is to say, each year, as part of your innovation meeting, you should also review what you implemented previously and what impact it had. Avoid the temptation to sugar coat or to ignore failures. It's the failures that offer the most opportunities to learn.

A SYSTEM FOR YOUR SYSTEMS

Engineering progress is the last step in the Build™ framework for a reason. The vast majority of service companies operate with inadequate systems at best, and no systems at worse.

The goal of this book and the goal of Build™ is to provide a framework for you to build a phenomenal company. But that's all that it is: a framework. A basis to start. A basic system that you can establish the foundation of your company on. This system works and it has been proven in multiple service companies that operate in multiple service categories.

Step 10 of the Build™ framework is the master step. It's the step that allows you to build on the framework. It's the system for maintaining and innovating your other systems. The first 9 steps of the

Build™ framework ask, "How do we do something right?" whereas step 10 asks a much more thoughtful and challenging question: "Are we doing the right things?"

Even though my wife and I were watering our plant and giving it plenty of sun, we completely missed the fact that the soil had to contain nutrients and food in order for the plant to survive and flourish. Likewise, your company needs systems and procedures, but without progress and innovation, you can literally die as a systematized and organized company. The key is to have a system to innovate your systems. That's exactly the purpose of step 10.

CHAPTER SUMMARY AND ACTION CHECKLIST

- Make room for failure. Allow yourself and your employees to fail in the pursuit of progress.
- Keep your eye on your vision at all times. As long as the things you do are in service to attaining your vision, your mistakes will not be made in vain.
- Adopting new technologies isn't always the answer. Make sure it's the right fit for you and your employees, and be honest with yourself if it isn't working.
- Invite your employees and customers to the innovation table. They will often bring different perspectives with them that can help you make the right choices for your unique company.
- Go to coalmarch.com/build to download the resources for this chapter.

"Life can only
be understood
backwards; but
it must be lived
forwards."

- Søren Kierkegaard

Chapter 16

The Mirror or the Window

My office at home is full of things that remind me of the high points in my career and my life. There are pictures of my wife, pictures of my kids, pictures of vacations we've taken as a family. There are also flags that I've flown in combat, my degree from North Carolina State University, and various medals I've earned as a pilot in the United States Air Force. In short, the photos and memorabilia in my office remind me of the rewards for doing hard things. I'm reminded of my life's journey so far, the sacrifices and the accomplishments, and where I want my journey to lead to in the future.

If you were to come into my office at home, you'd no doubt see that I am somewhat OCD about keeping things nice, organized, and neat. Each item that I mentioned above has a specific place in my office and everything is organized to keep the office neat and orderly.

But there's one object that on the surface looks hideous and very out of place on my desk. It's an old piece of plexiglass with a mirror film on it. On one side of the plexiglass you see only the mirror side of the film and on the other side you're able to peer through the tint to see what's on the other side.

This plexiglass mirror is about as ugly as they come. I made the mirror in a hurry in a Home Depot parking lot. I was in a hurry because each week our family has family night in which we play games, eat treats, and have a lesson. Guess whose turn it was to give the lesson that week?

The lesson I wanted to teach my kids was how selfishness distorts your vision of the world. I used my hack job plexiglass mirror that I built in the Home Depot parking lot to illustrate the point that you have completely different experiences depending on which side of the mirror you look into. On one side you see yourself and on the other side you see beyond yourself; you see what's out in the world. You see others. The idea behind the object lesson was that when you focus on yourself, that's all that you can see and you miss what's really going on around you. When you focus on others you can see opportunities and needs all around. What you choose to focus on is what makes the difference.

It was one of the very few lessons that I felt, as a dad, actually made an impact on my kids. To this day, my kids will sometimes ask the question, especially when someone is being particularly selfish, "Are you looking into the mirror or out the window?"

I kept the old piece of plexiglass because, as ugly and hacked up as it is, it still reminds me to not focus on myself so much that I end up missing what's happening around me. It's a reminder that my focus in life should be on what's happening outside of myself, not just on me. I also keep it around so that whenever my kids come into my office they're also reminded of its significance.

Though my kids don't know it yet, the plexiglass mirror is going to be used in another lesson when they get older. This time the mirror will have a new twist. While we all no doubt have the tendency to focus on ourselves, especially when we're young, we tend to reverse this impulse when it comes to doing hard things.

Most people, including myself, tend to have a very real and natural inclination to look through the mirror at other people, situations, and even circumstances when they fail to do something hard. The reality is that we should flip the mirror over and look at ourselves.

The lesson of the mirror is really two-fold. Lesson one is that happiness in life comes by looking through the mirror for opportunities to help others and to get outside of ourselves. Lesson two is that accomplishing hard things in life comes by building the habit of looking in the mirror, not through it.

As we close this book, I saved the most important concept for this final chapter. It's the lesson of the mirror. If you're truly serious about building a phenomenal company, you absolutely can do it. Thousands of people have, and thousands more will. Never in the history of the world has there ever been such an abundance of prosperity and opportunities.

As I mentioned earlier, business is nothing more than a game in which you have to satisfy the needs of the four main players: your customers, your employees, your vendors, and the owners. To build a truly phenomenal company, just apply the lesson of the mirror. Look through the mirror at the needs of these players and the "what" you should do as a company will become obvious.

I don't want to paint a rosy picture or set unrealistic expectations. Building a phenomenal company is very hard and will require giving your best to the effort. But, again if you apply the lesson of the mirror, what you should do will become glaringly obvious. Make no mistake, building a phenomenal company is hard. Look in the mirror. It all starts and ends with you. No one else is responsible, no one else is accountable. Avoid the temptation to blame situations, circumstances, and other people for why you can't do it.

While there are tons of books and programs out there that will berate you and give you "tough love" in the area of personal accountability, that's not the point I'm trying to make with the mirror.

The point that I am making is this: Everything in life is a system.

You, your family, your business, and even building your business, it's all a system. This book is about me sharing my system that I developed in growing multiple service companies. This system works. I personally use it and I have helped many others use it to build amazing companies. However, as great and effective that the system is, it's utterly worthless if you don't follow it and use it.

The real point is that the most critical element of the Build™ platform is you. It's up to you to decide if you're committed to building a phenomenal company. It's up to you to decide if you're willing to follow each step. Ultimately, no one and no system can build a phenomenal company for you. Look in the mirror, don't look through it.

I can personally attest to the benefits on the other side. Building a phenomenal company, while hard, is well worth the effort. You'll make more money and have more freedom than you've ever had, and most importantly you'll positively impact more people than you ever have. You can do all of those things if you're seriously committed to building a phenomenal company. All it takes is learning how to look into the mirror to get it done and how to look through the mirror to see the needs of others.

ORDER IN ALL THINGS

While I know that I stated this earlier in the book, it's so important that I am repeating it: The Build™ framework is designed to be done in the order it's presented. There's very good reasoning behind this.

Section 1 presents the idea that you must be motivated with the proper mindset to build a phenomenal company. That is, how to transition from the hero who's involved in the day-to-day operations of your business to a systems engineer who approaches your company from a strategic perspective. The idea is to see your business as one giant system composed of a collection of smaller integrated systems, and it's your responsibility to oversee them.

Section 2 covers each step of the Build™ platform. Notice how Steps 1-3 are all about getting clear on your vision of a phenomenal company. Before you build tracking systems, people systems, or even operational systems, you must know where you're going. Steps 4-10 cover how to build the systems that make your vision a reality. As a service company, your core systems are people systems because that's what you sell: human time and skill. These steps take you through the basic people systems of your service company and how to position your people to perform at their very best.

Section 3 of Build™ is all about the realization that you as an owner or manager are the most important element in the entire system.

DO THE HEAVY LIFTING FIRST

If you're out of your element when it comes to systems, procedures, and checklists, or if you're a little intimidated by the idea of creating a phenomenal company, don't let that stop you.

Go to the Coalmarch website, download the samples and templates, and start working. Accept the fact that your first round of this process is not going to be perfect, and that you'll make mistakes. Remember that failure is the price of innovation and progress. You'll never have systems and procedures that won't change or that don't need tweaking.

As you go through this process, you'll discover what really matters in building a great company. Oftentimes it's the knowledge you gain as you go through the business development process that allows you to spot and capitalize on opportunities in the moment. As with most things, the process is just as important as the result.

IF YOU WANT SOME HELP - COALMARCH

I've said a number of times that I own multiple service companies. One of them is Coalmarch, a professional people management and marketing company devoted to the success of other service companies. In other words, we're a company full of systems engineers.

By design, Coalmarch is built around the Build™ framework and Grow! IMS™, the proven digital marketing system I described in my first book of the same name. We are results-driven and work to help build phenomenal companies through recruiting, training, managing, marketing, and sales.

If you've read this far and feel you need help implementing the framework, go to coalmarch.com/build and request a free consultation. The Build™ platform can be implemented with this book and the worksheets provided, but there is help available if you need it. Just give us a call and we'll be happy to assist you.

LET'S STAY IN TOUCH

My goal in writing this book is to help you. Now you can do what most business owners just dream about: having a company that's phenomenal in every way.

This book describes the exact same system that I've used to build both of my service companies to the multi-million dollar level, and the same system that I use for our clients. I promise that if you take the time to implement this framework, your company will become a phenomenal company that provides phenomenal service with phenomenal people. It may not all happen at once, but I promise you, it will happen if you Build™ your company the right way.

I believe it's important to associate with and learn from those who are motivated to succeed. I would love to hear your experience and associate with you as you implement the Build™ framework.

Good luck and now go get to work! You can connect with me at:

email
dshelton@coalmarch.com
(note it may take a little time to respond as I travel frequently)

Twitter
@donnieray3

Facebook
https://www.facebook.com/donnie.r.shelton

CHAPTER SUMMARY AND ACTION CHECKLIST

- Only looking inward can distort your vision of the world. Look outside of yourself and consider the perspectives of your employees, customers, and peers. You'll have a better understanding of their needs and how you can fulfill them.
- Regularly assess your own strengths and weaknesses, and adjust your actions as needed. Be accountable for your own growth as well as that of your business.
- Take this framework one step at a time.
- You're not alone. There is help available for as little or as much of this process as you need.
- Go to coalmarch.com/build to download the resources for this chapter

Made in the USA
Columbia, SC
10 December 2020